Unlimited Intuition
NOW

Catherine Carrigan

Book design by RamaJon
Bikeapelli Press, LLC
Cover Photo by Catherine Carrigan

NOW Series Books are available for order through Ingram Press Catalogues

Catherine Carrigan
Visit my websites at
www.catherinecarrigan.com
www.unlimitedenergynow.com

Printed in the United States of America
First Printing: February 2016
ISBN: 978-0-9894506-1-4

TABLE OF CONTENTS

INTRODUCTION

Section I.

OPENING THE BOX OF MIRACLES

Section II.

THE OWNER'S MANUAL

Section III.

LISTENING WITH LOVE

Section IV.

CRUISING DOWN THE SPIRITUAL HIGHWAY

4

Section V.

ODE TO JOY

INTRODUCTION

Chapter 1: Christmas Eve

"Teach me your ways, Oh Lord;

make them known to me.

Teach me to live according to your truth,

for you are my God, who saves me.

I always trust in you."

Psalm 25

One Christmas Eve years ago, back in the day before cell phones when I used to walk around with a little less than

$2 in my wallet, I set off after work on a long drive to a family gathering 12 hours away in Virginia.

I had made it successfully out of Atlanta's heavy traffic, eaten a modest meal at a roadside restaurant someplace and was just settling in to the peace of a darkened interstate.

Suddenly, with no apparent warning, my old Acura stalled. I had just enough time to guide it safely to the side of the road.

"Dear God, please help me get to the next exit," I prayed.

I got out of my car, put on my hat, and as lickety-split as if I had just hailed a cab in Manhattan, an 18-wheeler pulled over just in front of me. It probably took only 45 seconds - - not long enough for me to get scared.

The cab door opened. A man and a woman waved me inside. Because there was a couple, I felt safe enough to get in. The trucker couple took me to the next exit.

It turned out that the husband had just left the hospital after throat surgery.

He was in tremendous pain, so being an energy healer and feeling extremely grateful for having been plucked off the side of the cold and lonely road, I spent an hour practicing hands-on healing for him in a fast-food restaurant at the exit.

About the time that the trucker's pain was completely gone, who should show up but my husband. He had left Atlanta about an hour behind me and had gone into a panic when he recognized my dirty white car in the dark by the side of the interstate.

My husband and the trucker then went back out into the dark night to get my old car running again.

I stayed behind at the restaurant and asked the wife for her mailing address -- someplace in Texas, if I recall.

Having grown up in the South, I had been well-trained to write thank-you notes for anyone who had done me a significant favor.

After Christmas passed and I got back to Atlanta, I wrote a two-page letter expressing how much I appreciated them rescuing me.

I double-checked the mailing address, licked the stamp and put the letter in my mailbox.

About six weeks later, the letter came back to me.

"Addressee unknown," the post office had stamped across the front.

It was right then and there that I knew I had been visited by angels.

Many people have never had the blessing of feeling lifted by an unseen hand.

Stranger still can be the surprise of receiving information out of the blue with no prior warning.

Chapter 2: Love Speaks Beyond All Time and Space

"The consciousness in you and the consciousness in me,

apparently two, really one, seek unity and that is love."

Nisargadatta Maharaj

One Sunday morning years ago, I went to church with my family over in South Carolina.

Suddenly and for no apparent reason, I felt overcome with grief and began to cry.

Yes, there are times in life when tears are meant to flow, but on this occasion I cried so much that soon enough water pooled on the wooden floor beneath my feet. For the life of me, I couldn't understand why.

Feeling embarrassed and confused, I left immediately after church to make the long drive back home to Atlanta.

Pretty much as soon as I got home, I received the call. My dear sweet grandmother had just passed away in a nursing home.

Had I known, I would have been with her, holding her hand, stroking her forehead and telling her just how much I loved her.

But I wasn't.

I had no idea and no clue about what was actually going on. As a result, she had been able to slip away without my loving interference.

Not thinking too clearly and still stuffed up with the grief that now had a name, I took out my journal and began to write.

Suddenly I heard her voice.

"Don't go," I pleaded.

"I will be with you in your writing," my grandmother replied.

I heard her voice as clearly as if she had been standing right next to me.

At the same time, I could feel the love we held for each other, embracing me and comforting me and reminding me that she would always be with me.

Chapter 3: Avoiding the Bomb

"Fairy tales are more than true: not because they tell us that dragons exist, but because they tell us that dragons can be beaten."

G.K. Chesterton

About 10 years after that, I had been visiting friends in London, England. I had gone into Covent Garden on a Wednesday morning, no problem.

The next day, a Thursday morning, I was due to travel back to the center of the city. But my guidance told me that if I got on the London Underground, I would have a hard time getting back.

I canceled my appointments and was taking a walk with suddenly nothing to do that morning when I came back to listen to the TV.

On that morning of July 7, 2005, four Islamic terrorists blew up the subway, then a bus. Fifty-two people died in the explosions and more than 700 were injured.

But me, I was out for a walk enjoying the sunshine.

To me, these stories have become almost ordinary. I could tell you nearly a hundred others just like them.

I've learned how to live my life by my guidance and taught many other people -- regular folks just like you -- how to do the same.

It is my prayer that as this book reveals itself to you, small miracles become commonplace as you learn to be guided by your own divine connection.

Section I.

OPENING THE BOX OF MIRACLES

Chapter 1: The Spiritual Faculty Called Intuition

"Go, go, go, said the bird: human kind

Cannot bear very much reality.

Time past and time future

What might have been and what has been

Point to one end, which is always present."

T.S. Eliot

Oftentimes, we want to know the end of the story, but the story hasn't finished being written yet.

Since before you were born, you have been accompanied by high-frequency beings commonly known as angels or spiritual guides.

They know you extremely well. In fact, they understand you so thoroughly they know ahead of time exactly how much of your story you can handle.

Have you ever had a friend whom you knew to be a little sensitive someone you had to be a little careful talking to?

So it is with us and our spiritual guides.

Your angels know exactly how much information you can handle at any one moment.

Maybe you don't need to hear that your divorce is actually going to take three years to wrap up instead of the six months you were hoping for.

You might get really upset if you knew it is going to take two years to sell your house instead of it flying off the market as you had hoped.

You may not be given the whole story when you ask for guidance, only the part you are psychologically equipped to handle.

Maybe you can handle knowing only your next step.

To expand your spiritual capacity, you can say a prayer:

HEAVENLY FATHER,

THANK YOU FOR PRESENTING ME WITH THE DEPTH AND QUALITY OF INFORMATION I AM CAPABLE OF HANDLING IN THIS MOMENT.

PLEASE STRENGTHEN ME ON ALL LEVELS.

GIVE ME THE GRACE TO ACCEPT WHAT I CANNOT CHANGE AND THE HUMILITY TO ALLOW WHAT I AM NOT ABLE TO DO ANYTHING ABOUT.

GIVE ME THE COURAGE TO HANDLE LIFE IN ALL ITS COMPLEXITY, TRIUMPHS AND TRIALS.

PLEASE EXPAND MY CAPACITY FOR KNOWING, FEELING, SEEING AND HEARING THE TRUTH IN ALL FORMS, IN ALL SITUATIONS, SO THAT I MAY BETTER SERVE YOU, GOD, ALL THE DAYS OF MY LIFE.

THANK YOU, GOD, THANK YOU, GOD,
THANK YOU, GOD.

AMEN.

Chapter 2: Ask for a Sign

"Ask the LORD your God for a sign, whether in the deepest depths or in the highest heights."

Isaiah 7:11

One of the simplest ways to engage your intuition is to ask for a sign.

Often we think that our guidance eludes us. You may think you have been forgotten, overlooked, that you don't matter, that nobody is looking out for you.

Nothing could be further from the truth.

Your guidance surrounds you all day long, every day, all the time, never leaving you, not even for one moment.

All you really have to do is open your psychic vision and see for yourself!

Here are two simple ways you can ask for a sign:

1. Go for a walk. This is one of my favorite ways to receive information. Say a prayer as you begin:

   DEAR GOD, I SEEK ADVICE, DIRECTION, INSIGHTS AND LEADERSHIP AT THIS TIME. PLEASE SHOW ME A SIGN. OPEN THE EYES OF MY SOUL THAT I MIGHT SEE THE ANSWERS. PLEASE MAKE THIS CLEAR AND EASY FOR ME.

   THANK YOU, GOD, THANK YOU, GOD, THANK YOU, GOD.

   AMEN.

   Notice what your eyes naturally zero in on. It could be a hawk circling in the sky. Maybe it's a dress hanging in the window. You may notice a feather lying in the street, a child babbling in a stroller or a throng of people arguing. Notice the pictures that naturally come to you. As you receive your symbol, welcome the image into your inner vision.

As you continue your walk, silently meditate on the meaning of what has been revealed to you. A hawk could be calling you to look at the larger picture. A dress hanging in the window could be asking you to change your costume, step out of your current drama and move into the next phase of your life. A feather lying in the street could ask you to be softer with yourself, gentler with all others. A child babbling in a stroller could be asking you to comfort your own inner child. A throng of people arguing could be warning you to avoid conflict. While you may be able to go home and look up the meaning of each symbol, take the picture inside yourself and notice what it means for you.

2. Pick up a few books or a stack of magazines. Allow yourself to pick up whichever book or magazine you seem most naturally drawn to. Don't think -- just pray and go. For example, you may say:

DEAR GOD, PLEASE GIVE ME INSIGHT ABOUT THE BEST WAY TO HANDLE THIS SITUATION. PLEASE SHOW ME THE WORDS, PHRASES OR PICTURES THAT WILL POINT ME IN MY BEST DIRECTION. PLEASE MAKE THE IMAGES CLEAR AND EASY FOR ME TO UNDERSTAND.

THANK YOU, GOD, THANK YOU, GOD, THANK YOU, GOD.

AMEN.

Holding your prayer in mind, flip open a page. Read, look, admire. Let the words and images on the page reveal themselves to you. If you feel confused, ask a clarifying question:

DEAR GOD, PLEASE SHOW ME THE NEXT STEP AFTER THAT.

Pick up the next book or magazine. Frankly, you could pick up a sacred text, such as the Bible, but for this exercise you will do equally well with *House Beautiful, Readers Digest* or *National Geographic.* Now take the words, phrases or images into your inner vision. Shut your eyes and contemplate the message you receive.

The gift of intuition may bless you with powerful symbols that convey feelings, energy and emotions beyond what words could ever express. However, you must still interpret the meaning of what you see, whether you spy a falling star, a crooked tree or a street full of cars and busy people.

Chapter 3: The Landscape of Easier Intuition

"Your soul knows when it's on to something."

Rachel Wolchin

You may notice that in certain locations you find it either easier or more difficult to access your intuitive guidance. For example, if you live in a large metropolitan area, such as London, Sydney, Beijing, Hong Kong, Toronto, New York, Tokyo or Paris, you may have a harder time accessing your psychic gifts.

Why is this the case?

When large numbers of people are gathered together in a condensed location, the combined negativity of all their fears, thoughts, beliefs and worries creates a cloud of psychic interference. In such places you are simply more easily influenced by other people's mental-emotional energy.

Even in Atlanta, where I live, the combined negativity in the city proper is greater than in the suburbs.

Living in such a situation, you have to be very clear in your own energy to maintain your divine connection, and there are things you can do to help this to happen.

Here is a simple way to determine your location's level of combined negativity:

Step One. Clear your energy. Pass your hands over your head three times. I usually say:

I CLEAR MY ENERGY IN THE NAME OF GOD THE FATHER, JESUS THE SON AND IN THE HOLY GHOST.

If you grew up in another spiritual tradition, simply choose words that feel right for you. Declare your intention to become totally clear of all negative interference.

Step Two. Ask for guidance. Size up your obstacles.

What is the combined negativity of my current location?

When I ask this question in the moment, here are the answers I receive for these urban areas:

Hong Kong: 51/100

Beijing: 50/100

Paris: 48/100

Tokyo: 46/100

New York: 43/100

London: 40/100

Toronto: 38/100

Sydney: 36/100

On the other hand, you may notice that it's much easier to access your intuition when you find yourself in nature.

On a mountaintop, you experience a natural uplift. Haven't you felt your spirit soar when you climbed to the top of a mountain, overlooking the valley below and seeing for miles around you?

In a valley, you may notice it's easier to go inside yourself.

At the beach, where the air is clear and heavily ionized, you may notice that your energy field, your aura, naturally expands.

Walking in the woods, where you are surrounded by trees and the sounds of birds and forest animals, you may find it much easier to access your inner quietude.

Towns of smaller populations may have less negative interference simply because fewer people are living together in a concentrated area.

When I ask for guidance about the level of negative interference in small towns, here is what I receive at the present moment:

Lyon, France: 17/100

Peterborough, Ontario, Canada: 14/100

Sedona, Arizona: 12/100

Isle of Gigha, Scotland: 12/100

Lhasa, Tibet: 11/100

If you've been living in a large city and finding it difficult to get in touch with your own inner guidance, here are a few steps you can take:

1. Get away to nature. Take a trip to the beach, hike up a mountain, walk in the woods. Get out of the city. If you can't get out, find your nearest city park and spend time walking or even sitting on a bench among the trees.

2. Clear your energy more frequently. Once you recognize you live in an area of dense population, you know you'll need to clear your energy so that you aren't affected by other people's thoughts and beliefs.

3. If you find yourself greatly disturbed by the psychic pressure of living in a large city, consider moving to a smaller town or even the countryside.

4. Use a flower essence for psychic protection. My favorite natural healing remedies for this purpose are Soul Shield+ by Living Tree Orchid Essences, Bubble from the Indigo Essences and Fringed Violet from the Australian Bush Flower Essences.

5. Cocoon yourself twice a day. You can read how in Section III, Chapter 10, later in this book

6. Meditate regularly to clear your mind. If you have a hard time meditating on your own, join a meditation group or visit a meditation center as you may find it easier to synchronize with the brain waves of other people in a clear state of mind.

7. If your profession requires you to deal with people who are highly stressed, such as nurses, doctors, police officers, ambulance workers, customer service representatives or the like, recognize that you may need to take additional steps to clear your energy throughout the workday to maintain your clear psychic channel.

8. Before you go to bed at night, set a glass of water beside your bed. Say a prayer and ask that all energies that come to you throughout the night be filtered through the water so that all you receive is peace, unconditional love and direct inspiration. In the morning, when you get up, don't drink the water. Throw it out.

9. Set up a peaceful sanctuary in your home. Create sacred space in whatever way feels most comfortable for you. You may include crystals such as amethyst, clear quartz, carnelian, kyanite and selenite, which clear energy. Include spiritual symbols such as a cross or pictures of saints. Say a prayer and ask that this room be a place of inner guidance for you and all who enter. Ask for angels to guard the room and surround it with the white light of protection.

10. Smudge your home and office by burning sage to clear out negative interference. Depending on where you live and work, you may need to do this regularly. Say a prayer and ask for angels to surround your home and office with the white light of protection and unconditional love.

Remember, environment is the most powerful factor in accessing your guidance. If you have trouble, ask yourself whether you are being negatively affected by your geographic location.

Chapter 4: How Outside Messages Differ from Your Own Intuition

"Intuition is the conception of an attentive mind, so clear, so distinct, and so effortless that we cannot doubt what we have so conceived."

René Descartes

As you open your sixth sense, you can begin sifting through the messages that actually come from your inner guidance as opposed to the voices of those around you:

- Your parents
- Your peers

- Your professors

- Your priests

- Your politicians

How can you tell if information doesn't come from your soul?

Your parents program your inner child. People are most easily imprinted with beliefs before the age of five, and many of the ideas you have about yourself came from what you interpreted your parents to say to you at that early age.

Counsel you receive from your parents includes all your little-kid beliefs:

- You are/are not good enough

- You are/are not beautiful/handsome

- You are/are not smart

- You are/are not lovable

Your peers are your sparring partners. They provide messages for who you are today:

- You do/do not fit in

- You do/do not matter

- How you must talk/act/look to be part of the crowd

Your professors give you a map for the world around you:

- How the world supposedly is/is not

- What is/is not true

- How things are/are not supposed to be done

- How things do/do not work

Your priests instruct your moral guidelines:

- What is/is not right/wrong

- How you are/are not supposed to act

- What you must do/not do to be right with God

Your politicians inform the rules about the country you live in:

- What you can/cannot do

- Where you can/cannot go

- Who you can/cannot be

- What you can/cannot say

If you think through all the messages that your parents, peers, professors, priests and politicians give you, there is a degree of outside control in what they are communicating.

Your inner messages stand apart because rather than trying to control you, your soul wants to liberate you.

No one else has a life purpose quite like yours.

No one can do what you alone are meant to do.

Rather than telling you what *not* to be, think, wear, eat, say or do, your soul will be prompting you to reach for your greatest joy.

If you find yourself feeling overwhelmed, complete the following exercise:

Step One. Write down what you think your parents want you to do, be or have.

Step Two. List what you think your peers would like you to do, be or have.

Step Three. Jot down the messages from all the people who have ever trained, educated or instructed you about what you are supposed to do, be or have.

Step Four. Scribble down what the people in your church, synagogue or mosque have to say about the subject.

Step Five. Finally, make note of your country's laws.

As you write down the prescriptions from your parents, peers, professors, priests and politicians, how do you feel? As you filter everybody else out, the rest is you.

As your emotions come up, notice your soul longing.

Underneath all the commandments, what would you rather experience?

That would be your soul talking.

Uncluttered.

Uncensored.

Maybe you get a simple picture, a word, a sensation, an inner knowing. That's your soul speaking its simple truth, your sacred key to unlock your future.

Give yourself permission now to act from this place of inner knowing.

Chapter 5: Don't Be Afraid, It's Only Your Angels

"I have come to drag you out of yourself and take you in my heart.

I have come to bring out the beauty you never knew you had and lift you like a prayer to the sky."

Jalāl ad-Dīn Muhammad Rūmī

From time to time over the years, as I've taught clients how to communicate first and then deepen the channel of their angelic communication, I've met people whose fear gets in the way.

"Don't be afraid," I reassure them. "Your angels love you!"

The two biggest emotions that arise when fearing angels include:

1. Guilt

2. Unworthiness

Guilt. Yes, you have made a few mistakes -- maybe even more than a few mistakes. You've made choices that you knew to be wrong, and now you feel more than a little ashamed.

You can let go of your primal guilt by recognizing that your mistakes didn't even start with you.

Stretching back over the millennia, your ancestors made quite a few errors of judgment so egregious that their poor choices even led to their own deaths as well as the loss of many other lives.

Just as you carry this primal guilt in your DNA as a consequence of being born a human, you as a soul also carry a true innocence. You've made soul contracts with other souls throughout this and many other lifetimes.

Often you may not actually comprehend what these apparent and so-called mistakes were all about -- who taught you what, how another soul grew or deepened their God connection as a result of your apparently ill-timed actions.

The truth is you don't even have to understand any of it.

Use this simple forgiveness mantra if you feel too guilty to receive angelic guidance:

I FORGIVE (YOUR NAME).

(YOUR NAME) FORGIVES ME.

I LOVE (YOUR NAME).

(YOUR NAME) LOVES ME.

Repeat this forgiveness mantra over and over until you feel the counterproductive energy of guilt has lifted from your soul.

Guilt has a specific heavy density. You will know when you have cleared your guilt because you will feel noticeably lighter.

Unworthiness. You may not feel worthy to receive the time and attention of an actual angel. After all, you are not a big shot. Maybe you don't have a big job, a big life, a big anything.

Please know that just by virtue of having a body in this lifetime, you have already been incredibly blessed. Even if you don't know how or why, even if you have no clue about your purpose, keep in mind that because you are born, you are cherished. Your angels want to help you succeed.

You can clear your own feelings of unworthiness with the simple process that follows.

But first, be sure to understand that to feel worthy, you don't have to change anything. You don't need to be taller, shorter, richer, poorer, better-looking, change the style of your hair, get more well-versed at social media, read more spiritual books, acquire any degrees, stop swearing, clean up your act or make one iota of shift to who you really are.

There will never be another person exactly like you anywhere on the planet. You are meant to be you in this lifetime and nobody else.

So, feeling worthy isn't about changing your outward appearance or your inner character. All you really have to do is be you, offering your specific vibration to the planet.

As an energy healer myself, I think in terms of energies. Every person, place or thing has a specific vibration.

You are already a VIP -- a vibrational interference pattern. Your vibration is as specific and as unique to you as your fingerprint.

So here's how you get over feeling unworthy to receive guidance, communicate with your angels or receive the best-quality guidance of anybody coming down the pike.

Use this prayer:

HEAVENLY FATHER,

PLEASE HELP ME TO FEEL THE UNCONDITIONAL LOVE ALL AROUND ME.

PLEASE OPEN MY EYES TO SEE HOW MY OUTWARD EXPERIENCE IS A DIRECT REFLECTION OF THE QUALITY OF MY INNER THOUGHTS.

GIVE ME THE COURAGE NOW TO EMBRACE WHO I AM ON ALL LEVELS.

EMBOLDEN ME TO STEP INTO MY SPIRITUAL PURPOSE.

THANK YOU FOR ALL I EXPERIENCE.

THANK YOU, ANGELS, SPIRITUAL GUIDES AND ALL THE HEAVENLY HOSTS, FOR SUPPORTING ME, LOVING ME AND GUIDING ME ALL THE DAYS OF MY LIFE.

REMIND ME WHY I AM GOOD ENOUGH, HOW I WAS BORN GOOD ENOUGH, HOW I HAVE ENOUGH AND WHY I AM ENOUGH.

I NOW HUMBLY ACCEPT THE DIVINE GUIDANCE THAT IS MY BIRTHRIGHT AS A CONSEQUENCE OF BEING BORN A HUMAN.

THANK YOU, GOD, THANK YOU, GOD, THANK YOU, GOD.

AMEN.

Chapter 6: Three Lies Your Ego Likes to Tell You

"You were wild once. Don't let them tame you."

Isadora Duncan

One of the major sources of interference to quality guidance from your soul comes from your ego.

What is your ego?

Your ego could be defined as your mind.

This mind of yours has decided who it thinks you are.

Because the ego is ruled by fear, more than likely your ego has set limits on who you think you are, what you think you deserve to experience in this lifetime and what you think you are capable of accomplishing.

As Henry Ford once said, "If you think you can do a thing or think you can't do a thing, you're right."

Meanwhile, your soul has messages it wants to share with you, such as

- "Go HERE."
- "The opportunities are over THERE."
- "This person can help you, but that one doesn't really care."
- "Your real talent is X."

Your soul has truly important information to share because it sees, hears, feels and knows from a totally expansive perspective.

This soul guidance is sometimes called psychic information, angelic communication, or divine direction. You could call it your gut feeling, your inner knowing, your sixth sense.

This high-quality information can come to you -- but only if you get your ego out of the way long enough for these hints to drop in.

Here are three lies your ego likes to tell you:

Ego Lie Number One. That it's important for you to judge everything and everyone. When you judge, your ego mind puts labels on things: "This is terrible for me, this is really wonderful." Your ego likes to categorize people, places and events. Personally, I like to think of a spectrum with judgment on one end and divine guidance on the other, just like the range of visible light from red to blue. When you judge anyone or anything, you immediately shut down your soul communication because you've put the experience in a box that fails to acknowledge the actual limits to your understanding. Even scientists report that only 4 percent of the known universe is visible. The other 96 percent can't be seen, comprehended or detected.

What if your ego actually knows nothing, in which case you'd be better off asking your soul for guidance from an expanded perspective? What if, however, everything that ever happened to you was for your highest best interests? What if there are no mistakes? What if you made soul agreements before you were born so that everything works out for the highest good of all concerned?

Ego Lie Number Two. That you don't matter, that you are too small/insignificant/unimportant, the wrong gender, the wrong color, the wrong age, or in the wrong country to make a difference, so why bother? When you think small, you fail to value your life and the importance of your own choices. Quantum physics likes to talk about the butterfly effect. That is, a small change in initial conditions in one state of a nonlinear system can result in large differences in a later state. Additionally, merely observing a phenomenon will change that phenomenon. You matter. What you think and do matters. Your being changes everything everywhere. When you recognize your connection to the whole, ask for guidance about how you can contribute at a higher level.

Ego Lie Number Three. That you need to stay safe. You will be alive in this body in this lifetime until you aren't. In physics, the law of conservation of energy states that energy can neither be created nor destroyed. What appears to be "destruction" is simply energy transforming from one state to another. Your ego arranges your entire thought structure around the myth that the world out there might possibly be scary, threatening or dangerous. Einstein said, "I think the most important question facing humanity is, 'Is the universe a friendly place?' This is the first and most basic question all people must answer for themselves."

When you behave as if the entire game has been rigged for your highest good, knowing that you can't really make any mistakes, you can give yourself permission to ask for guidance about which risks to take.

Guidance happens when we create the space in our minds to allow our angels to speak up. Set your ego aside and listen!

Chapter 7: Your Soul Longing

"I know nothing with any certainty, but the

sight of stars makes me dream."

Vincent Van Gogh

Many people believe they aren't intuitive, that they don't have any psychic gifts at all and that the woo-woo stuff is for somebody else much weirder than they are.

Personally, I don't believe that is the case. From having worked with all kinds of people over the years, I believe you are intuitive even if you haven't yet recognized exactly how you receive your information. You have intuitive gifts because you have a soul.

I believe you always have access to your intuitive gifts if you just stop long enough to pay attention.

You can be trained to learn how to operate these gifts and use them for your own benefit as well as possibly blessing the lives of others:

Your **clairaudience**, hearing without sound, is your soul's way of deep listening.

Your **claircognizance**, knowing without prior evidence, is your soul's way of understanding the world.

Your **clairsentience**, feeling the energy and emotions around you, is your soul's way of picking up the vibe.

Your **clairvoyance**, seeing what's not visible to your naked eye, is your soul's map of the universe.

Even if you never learn about any of these gifts, you can get in touch with your intuition by paying attention to your soul longing.

Here's a simple exercise.

Get out a sheet of paper and a pen or pencil.

Write down three questions at the top of the piece of paper:

1. What does my soul long for me to *do* today?

2. What does my soul long for me to *have* this week?

3. What does my soul long for me to *be* this year?

Ideally, you want to write this by hand as opposed to using a computer so that there is no electronic interference. But if you have only a tablet, smart phone, laptop or desktop, those will do.

Give yourself no more than five minutes and write as quickly as you can.

Don't censor yourself. Just write what comes to you.

When you answer the question about what your soul longs to *do* today:

- You get in touch with the activities that will bring you the greatest joy.

- You discover how you can take steps toward your life purpose.

- You align with your spiritual direction.

When you answer the question about what your soul longs to *have* this week:

- You know the materials and resources you need to be happiest.

- You discover the tools necessary to serve at the highest level.

- You make it easier to flow with what's coming up for you because you are prepared.

When you answer the question about what your soul longs to *be* this year:

- You feel, visualize, hear and know how to express your highest potential.

- You direct yourself to be the best you can be.

- You embody your soul's expression.

In short, you can get in touch with your intuition simply by asking yourself what your soul longs for you to do, have and be -- that's it! No "woo-woo" instruction required!

As you complete this exercise, you may surprise yourself.

Go ahead, feel surprised and then give yourself permission to move forward. In this simple way, you may uncover great intuition about yourself because your soul is always directing you forward and onward into the light of happiness.

Section Two:

THE OWNER'S MANUAL

Chapter 1: Ask to See With Your Soul

"You will receive power when the Holy Spirit comes upon you."

Acts 1:8

Many times we hope to gain deeper insight, but the ego stops us.

The truth is that the world most of us experience is the drama we project from inside of us to the outside. Our inner experience plays the role of movie projector, and the outer macrocosm becomes the screen.

If you feel confused and want to know how you really feel inside, ask yourself, "What do I notice most often in life around me?"

When we feel angry, we look outside ourselves and discover 100 new reasons to be angry.

When grief engulfs us, the world plays tragedy for us.

When fear shakes us, nothing outside anywhere looks secure. The stock market tumbles, the news reinforces our uncertainty. Nobody can really be trusted.

At times like this, viewing life from our inner movie projected outward, it's so easy for us to lose hope.

And yet somewhere inside, despite the anger, the grief and the anxiety, you always have hope.

You can ask to see with your soul.

Here is a simple prayer you can say:

DEAR GOD,

THANK YOU SO MUCH FOR THE GIFT OF MY LIFE.

THANK YOU FOR THE PRIVILEGE OF BEING IN THIS BODY IN THIS LIFETIME.

THANK YOU FOR ALL MY BLESSINGS, EVEN IF I AM HAVING TROUBLE SEEING OR EXPERIENCING THE DEPTH AND FULLNESS OF ALL OF THEM AT THIS TIME.

PLEASE HELP ME NOW TO SEE WITH MY SOUL.

GIVE ME THE COURAGE, THE INSIGHT AND THE WILLINGNESS TO ACCESS THE WISDOM OF MY ETERNAL BEING.

PLEASE GUIDE ME SO THAT I EXPERIENCE THE BEAUTY AND WONDER OF THIS LIFE YOU HAVE BLESSED ME WITH.

I NOW SURRENDER MY WILL TO YOUR WILL, GOD.

PLEASE HELP ME TO SET ASIDE MY EGO MIND SO THAT I MAY KNOW WHAT YOU WOULD HAVE ME KNOW, GOD.

PLEASE WIPE AWAY MY TROUBLED EMOTIONS SO THAT I MAY FEEL WHAT YOU WOULD HAVE ME FEEL, GOD.

PLEASE TUNE MY HEARING SO THAT I MAY HEAR THE HIGHEST AND BEST VIBRATIONS.

PLEASE OPEN MY VISION FAR AND WIDE SO THAT I MAY SEE WITH THE TRUE DEPTH AND DETAIL THAT YOU WOULD HAVE ME SEE, GOD.

THANK YOU FOR BLESSING ME WITH THIS NEW VISION, SO THAT I MAY KNOW, FEEL, HEAR AND SEE FROM THE HIGHEST POSSIBLE PERSPECTIVE.

MAKE ME YOUR SERVANT IN ALL WAYS.

PLEASE GUIDE ME IN EVERY ASPECT OF MY LIFE SO THAT I MAY BRING OUT THE BEST IN MYSELF AND ALL OTHERS.

THANK YOU, GOD, THANK YOU, GOD, THANK YOU, GOD.

AMEN.

As you begin to see with your soul, you open up your highest intuitive gifts. You know, you feel, you hear and you see how the cosmos blesses everyone as it unfolds.

When we see from this higher perspective, the truth often reveals that life has actually always been the opposite of what we experienced: guided, loved unconditionally and never actually alone.

Many people think that opening your intuition is about acquiring special powers. More likely, seeing with your soul will bless you with greater capacity for awe and wonder, for joy and appreciation of all the quiet miracles that happen around us every day when we stop to look and admire.

Open your intuition and reveal the joy of your life to yourself and all others!

Chapter 2: Three Good Reasons to Use Your Psychic Gifts for Your Own Personal Benefit

"Listen to your own Self.

If you listen to that Self within, then you find the Truth."

Kabir Das

Whether your primary psychic gift is **clairsentience, claircognizance, clairvoyance** or **clairaudience**, you will want to use these gifts for yourself. Why is it so important that you use these senses for yourself?

These gifts are your soul trying to communicate with you. Recently, I had tea with a highly sensitive person. She told me she would see colors and pick up feelings when she worked with people. Her friends had advised her to shut down this information. "No," I said. "The people who are advising you actually don't know the truth. This is your soul trying to communicate with you. If you try to shut off the messages of your soul, the pressure will only build up, you will feel even more uncomfortable and your soul will simply try to get through to you in multiple other ways." We have to recognize that our soul is actually in charge -- not our ego. Your soul has an important mission and will speak loudly if you are going off course. I always say, "When you are paying attention, God only has to tap you on the shoulder." Why wait for the sledgehammer approach?

If you use your intuitive gifts primarily for other people and not for yourself, you can develop a serious energy imbalance. Frankly, it's helpful for intuitive people to have friends who have learned how to manage their psychic gifts successfully. I say if you own a Ferrari -- a very fast vehicle -- you better learn how to drive it or you can get in trouble in a hurry. If you are a highly sensitive person, find other highly sensitive people who have become strong enough to handle their sensitivity. You probably don't want to feel crazy most of the time, I would assume, no? So here's the truth. When other people discover you are psychic, they will sometimes treat you like a psychic Pez dispenser. I kid you not, I had one person phone me in the middle of the night from Saudi Arabia. Because I was asleep and assumed it must be an emergency for someone to call at that hour, I stupidly answered the phone. When I tried to explain the time difference, that didn't stop the lady from demanding instant information. Fortunately, I have enough personal boundaries that I refused. That is one way we can be drained, but here is another. If you use your gifts for others and not for yourself, you will end up feeling exhausted and not be able to put your finger on why you are so tired. Putting it positively: When you listen to your soul and follow your own guidance, you will fill yourself up energetically. Feeling drained is a good sign that you aren't listening and have gotten off course. I can tell you from personal experience that you must use your gifts primarily for yourself -- more for yourself even than for others -- or you will end up being very drained, and no amount of nutritional supplements, Reiki, qi gong, yoga, meditation, prayer, vacation or other therapies will fix the problem.

Your soul can feel, know, see and hear far beyond the capacity of your fingers, your brain, your eyes and your ears. It provides high-quality information. Because 96 percent of the known universe cannot be measured or quantified in any way, you will want to dive into this qualitative, subtle, substantial, mysterious and often initially unsubstantiated guidance and at the least get very curious about it. Why did you just get told to take a left and not a right? Why did you hear you were supposed to stay home and not get on that plane? Why did you get the hint that you are better off going out on a limb, moving to another state, taking another job or doing something entirely different? Maybe you aren't totally crazy -- maybe there are huge opportunities for you if you take advantage of them.

As a medical intuitive healer, I use my gifts in my work all day long. But I also use them to know when to go to the store to find the right shoes on sale, when to stop what I am doing even if I have been wildly successful up to that point, when to buy a house, whom to hire, when to move on and more.

You can become more proficient in building this open soul communication if you start with yourself first. Then, as you build your confidence, you can take your gifts into your work and discover a whole new level of mastery.

Chapter 3: Discover the Golden Egg of Your Own Intuition

"Understanding was coming so fast, it seemed to bypass thought."

J.K. Rowling

Sometimes people ask me when I first discovered my intuition. I could go back and back into time, but here's the first story I can remember.

When I was growing up, my family lived in England. Specifically, we lived in Hampstead (right outside of London), where my father was completing his residency as an eye surgeon. At the time, I was six years old and my little brother was almost three.

In April of that year, when it came time for my little brother to celebrate his third birthday, my parents decided to host an Easter egg hunt for the local children. The eggs -- including a golden egg -- were carefully hidden in our back garden.

During the hiding of the eggs, my brother and I were instructed to hide inside the house, which we did.

But there was much discussion in the house about the golden egg -- a Cadbury chocolate egg wrapped in gold foil paper.

On the day of my little brother's party, all of us kids were kept in the house and at a certain time the glass doors were opened and we were all let out into the back garden to hunt for our eggs. The other little children went running hither and yon, carrying their egg baskets.

I remember walking directly to a large tuft of tall grass and immediately picking up the golden egg, first thing, unprompted, within maybe 60 seconds of being let out into the back garden.

What followed was a series of recriminations. My parents accused me of watching while they hid the eggs. That actually wasn't true.

Even though it wasn't true and even though I wasn't then and am still not a liar, I got spanked anyway (I was always getting spanked).

Accessing our intuition is just like this.

You focus, and the truth is revealed, even if you can't actually see the golden egg hidden in the tall grass.

It was many years afterwards -- decades in fact -- before I recognized that I had used my intuition at my little brother's birthday party. In a way, though, that's OK because the story shows that I have always been intuitive and that I must have been born this way. Indeed, the "golden egg" was not the Cadbury chocolate kind -- no matter how yummy -- but rather recognizing this gift in myself.

Do you have a golden egg inside of you? You are about to find out!

Chapter 4: What Is Clairaudience?

"In many shamanic societies, if you came to a medicine person complaining of being disheartened, dispirited, or depressed, they would ask one of four questions: When did you stop dancing? When did you stop singing? When did you stop being enchanted by stories? When did you stop finding comfort in the sweet territory of silence?"

Gabrielle Roth

Clairaudience is your gift of psychic hearing.

Strengths:

- Receives information through sounds, vibration, unspoken words and even music

- Best gift for channeling

- Ideal for public speakers to express what needs to be heard

- Allows you to connect to your inner voice

- Empowers you to listen to your angels

- Like the gift of claircognizance, comes in very fast

- Gives you the power to write from your soul, not just from your ego

- Can be healed by sound and music

- Clear and direct

- Like clairsentience, picks up the vibration of situations, as all sound is a vibration

- Best gift for quick and sudden warnings, *e.g.*, hearing an inner voice cry "Watch out!"

- Capable of telepathic communication

- Can hear others' thoughts

- Can be healed by sound

Weaknesses:

- You may think what you hear are your own thoughts rather than divine guidance

- May be so sensitive to vibration you can be affected by extremely low frequency (ELF) vibrations

- Information comes so fast you may speak bluntly and brusquely unless you slow down to consider how to express yourself in a kind and thoughtful manner

- Can be overloaded with too many thoughts and words all at once

- You or others may think you are crazy from hearing voices in your head

- Hypersensitive to noise and even high-intensity light vibrations

Energy center for receiving clairaudience:

- 5th chakra

What helps you develop your clairaudience:

- Meditation

- Sitting quietly

- Time alone to listen to your guidance

- Using tuning forks to balance the sound energy in the body

- Singing and vocal toning

- Listening to Solfeggio harmonics, the frequencies of Gregorian chants

- Listening to all kinds of music

- Automatic writing by typing or scribbling so fast you outpace your ego mind

- Asking your angels to speak to you and writing down what they say

- Paying attention when thoughts, words or guidance suddenly appear to drop in

- Affirm: I HEAR THE DEEPER MEANING IN ALL SITUATIONS

- Affirm: I LISTEN DEEPLY TO THE VOICES OF ALL MY ANGELS

I remember years ago working with a client with life-long back pain due to polio as a child. Because he was an ordained minister, at first I thought he wouldn't be open to healing work, much less the full range of all I had to offer.

As it turned out, he was so determined to get better he was open to everything I had to say. Probably the fact that he saw himself getting better helped!

One day he was having a particularly hard time, and I did a healing with him.

It turned out he was being affected by earthquakes in South America (I kid you not).

Even I had a hard time understanding that one at first, except I understood that his primary psychic gift was clairaudience. He was a powerful public speaker and intuitively understood how to speak from his soul.

Meanwhile, he was so sensitive to vibration that his physical body reacted to the earth shaking even continents away.

Personally, I love the blessing of my clairaudience because it makes my healing work so much easier.

"It's the foot," I will hear my angels directing me.

Why waste time figuring things out when I can simply listen?

As an author, I use this gift when I write. I literally wait until I hear what to write about.

I may be sound asleep, then get awakened in the middle of the night and hear the title of a chapter or a phrase about a certain topic.

Sometimes I simply pray for guidance until I hear what to write about, then I get on my laptop and allow the words to pour forth.

For years, even at college, I remember being confused when I heard of other writers who were "finding their inner voice."

I never needed to "find" my voice – mine practically never shuts up!

Because I know I am high in the gift of claircognizance and clairaudience, the two fastest of all the psychic gifts, I frequently receive a complete download of information and then have to pause and consider how to relate what I have been gifted with so that I can express myself kindly to my clients.

I frequently warn my clients, "I am nice but blunt. Please understand that I am speaking for your highest good and have no intention of hurting your feelings in any way."

One of my most powerful experiences of clairaudience came years ago.

I had been very sick for about a month, but one morning I woke up and could literally hear my angels singing a Gregorian chant inside my head.

At that point, I knew I was well and that my illness had left me for good. I felt as joyous as my angels singing anthems of praise and thanksgiving!

Chapter 5: What Is Claircognizance?

"All things are connected like blood which unites one family."

Chief Seattle

Claircognizance is your psychic gift of inner knowing.

Strengths:

- Fastest of all the psychic gifts

- Comes to you with little or no supporting information

- Blesses you with information on subjects you know nothing about

- Great for advance warnings

- Gets the big picture

- Often referred to as the prophetic gift, as it gives you the power to predict, foresee and forecast

- Good for knowing others' advance moves

- Ideal for personal protection to keep you out of dangerous situations

- Ability to project your energy into any person, place or situation to know what is going on

- You see the truth in situations despite how other people present themselves

- Best psychic sense for solving problems

- Other people come to you for advice because you just know what they can't figure out

- Very curious about the world, open to all kinds of information, loves to learn

- Good for reading the Akashic Records, a compendium of thoughts, emotions and events encoded in the non-physical plane

- Ability for astral projection (or out-of-body experiences)

- Can sense the world from both a micro and macro perspective, such as seeing organs within a body or viewing the world from street level

- Spots opportunities ahead of time

- Ability to communicate with angels and spiritual guides

Weaknesses:

- Comes to you with either no supporting information or so little you may question yourself or others may question you

- Often gets information way ahead of time, before you are prepared to deal with it

- So fast you may have to pay more attention to the timing

- You can be flooded with ideas and information

- You have to slow down to communicate with others

- People may think you are crazy or wrong because what you talk about hasn't happened yet

- You may appear brash or rude because you speak bluntly and directly

- Tends to be ungrounded and have trouble connecting to the earth

- Easy for others to dismiss the information because it comes to you so quickly and easily

Energy center for receiving claircognizance:

- 7th chakra

- All chakras above the crown of your head

What helps to develop your claircognizance:

- Meditation

- Any activity that clears the mind to make space for your intuitive guidance to drop in

- Brain integration work (to integrate the right and left hemispheres of your brain)

- Deep relaxation

- Getting into neutral, so you can get your ego mind out of the way

- Grounding activities, such as walking barefoot

- Energy exercises such as yoga, tai chi or qi gong that open the crown chakra

- Prayer and deep spiritual work

- Getting off psychiatric medications, which cloud your mind

- Setting your intention to align your will with divine will

Affirm: EVERYTHING I NEED TO KNOW COMES TO ME BY GRACE IN PERFECT TIME

Affirm: I KNOW WHAT I NEED TO KNOW WHENEVER I NEED TO KNOW IT

When I first began studying healing work, my mentor in healing sent me to a woman who helps people identify their psychic gifts.

When you practice healing work, it's important for you to understand how you receive information so you don't second-guess yourself.

Frankly, whatever you do, if you understand how you receive extraordinary information, you will be much better off!

Discovering that my primary psychic gift is claircognizance gave me a huge "aha!" moment. Suddenly so many things about myself made perfect sense.

I understood why I had been Phi Beta Kappa at Brown University, but also why I need time alone to process all the many thoughts that come to me.

It suddenly made sense why I could stay out dancing the night before a test and then ace the exam.

The lady who taught me about my own psychic gifts explained that her husband, a mechanic, is also high in claircognizance.

People would bring their rare antique automobiles to him. Instead of taking the engine apart, he would simply imagine the apparatus in his mind and mentally go straight to the problem. Then he would actually do the work and fix it.

If claircognizance is your primary psychic gift, slow down to learn how to operate it so you can enjoy being fast, thinking fast and living fast!

Chapter 6: What Is Clairsentience?

"If you sense there must be more, there is more."

Alan Cohen

Clairsentience is your psychic gift of feeling.

Strengths:

- Able to read the energy and emotions of others

- Best psychic gift for picking up the vibe of any situation

- Can read temperature, texture and the sensations of any person, place or thing.

- Great for reading the chi in different body organs

- Ideal gift for massage therapists, Reiki masters and energy healers

- Sensitive to the emotional state of others and able to respond appropriately.

- Good for knowing how to act in social situations

- Makes you a great people person because you intuitively understand others

- Improves sales performance as you can feel the buyer's opinions

- Best for hiring the right person for the job

- Able to perform psychometry, *i.e.,* reading information by picking up objects owned by others

- Naturally good with animals, small children and people not able to communicate through ordinary methods

- Kind, naturally compassionate and thoughtful

- Best psychic gift for feng shui, *i.e.,* arranging a home or office to balance the energy flow

- Able to understand the psychological challenges of an individual or group

- Empathetic and empathic

- One of the easiest psychic gifts to develop

Weaknesses:

- Confusion about whether how you feel is your actual emotion or the energy and reactions of other people

- Can easily take on other people's energy and emotions without realizing it

- May have weak psychic boundaries

- Unsure of your own thoughts and feelings

- Need other people to be "up" so you can feel good, too

- Need to maintain a high vibration yourself so you don't become a magnet for negativity

- Your mood can quickly shift because you pick up the energy around you

- Low self-esteem unless you develop a strong sense of yourself

- You'll need to interpret the energy and emotions you pick up

- Nonverbal, qualitative gift

- May have difficulty being in crowds

- Can take on others' pain and suffering

- Easily influenced by others' thoughts and opinions

- Codependent

- Overly sensitive

- Emotional basket case

- May have digestive disorders and upset stomach due to overactive 3rd chakra

- The slowest of all the psychic gifts

Energy center for receiving clairsentience:

- 3rd chakra.

What helps to develop your clairsentience:

- Spend time alone at least three times a day to ask yourself how you feel

- If your energy or emotion shifts after that, ask if you have picked up the vibe from somebody else

- Wear purple bracelets on your wrists to keep from picking up energy from others, especially if you practice hands-on healing

- Cocoon yourself to protect your energy

- Pick up an object owned by somebody else and read the story it has to tell

- Place your hands on a body and set your intention to feel the chi in various organs

- Pray to be drawn to the highest vibration location in any office, room or home

- Feel the beat of music

- Bring your hands to face each other about 12 inches apart, feeling the soft cotton-like energy between them

- Practice tai chi and qi gong

- Walk on the beach to feel your own energy field expand

- Take a hot bath with equal parts Epsom salt and baking soda to clear your energy field daily, especially if you have a job working with the public, such as sales, teaching, healing work or psychotherapy

- Practice getting into neutral, where your own emotions step out of the way

- Pay attention to your gut feelings

- Value your own emotional intelligence

- Give yourself time to feel all your emotions

- Take good care of your digestion, learning what foods agree with your body and slowing down to eat your meals in a relaxed setting

- Do not eat when you feel upset or you will mix the bad emotions into your food and have difficulty digesting

- When you are getting dressed, look at your clothes and ask what you need to wear to feel comfortable throughout the day

- If you find yourself around negativity, visualize a fire hydrant at your 3rd chakra projecting energy outward so you don't take anything on

- Visualize a person, place or thing in your own 3rd chakra to analyze how they feel

- Project your energy ahead into your day to notice how you will feel in each planned event

- Affirm: I HAVE NOTHING TO GIVE OR RECEIVE EXCEPT UNCONDITIONAL LOVE

- Affirm: NOTHING COMES IN AND NOTHING GOES OUT OF MY ENERGY FIELD EXCEPT UNCONDITIONAL LOVE

It's my experience that people high in the psychic gift of clairsentience are some of the sweetest people you will ever meet.

I have never seen a single one of my clairsentient clients ever intentionally hurt anybody else. They are so dialed in to the energy and emotions of others that they naturally know how to act, what to say and how to uplift everybody else.

Their downside can be that they don't think they are very smart and can tend to have low self-esteem, but I always assure them that in my mind emotional intelligence is the most valuable gift.

Although I myself as a prophetic person high in claircognizance am very fast, I always tell my "feeler" clients that fast isn't necessarily better, it's just a speed like a setting on your washing machine.

Slow or fast, you can still get the job done!

If clairsentience is your primary psychic gift, take time to appreciate yourself for the kindness you contribute to the world.

Chapter 7: What Is Clairvoyance?

"I shut my eyes in order to see."

Paul Gaugin

Clairvoyance is your gift of psychic vision.

Strengths:

Ability to read the energy field or aura around a person

Receives information through symbols, images and pictures in your mind's eye

Capacity to project your energy into other locations around the globe for remote viewing

Foresight to "see ahead" into future events and situations

Retroactive vision to witness details of past events and situations

May catch glimpses of sequential actions

Ideal for spotting fashion trends

Understands the symbology and psychology of color

Great for creating the ideal appearance to fit in to any group or situation

Best for decorating a space and knowing how to lay out any environment

Helps you find lost items

Capacity to shift perspective, such as when you narrow your inner vision to inspect things up close (*e.g.,* looking inside the body's organs) or expand to get a wider view (*e.g.,* observing a building from street level)

May receive images in a dream or daydream

Good at tracking nature's messages

Makes it easier to manifest what you want because you have the capacity to visualize the end result

Sees beyond appearances to what is really going on

Visionary to see what's really needed

Photographic memory

Ability to see angels

Weaknesses:

Tendency to get stuck on a specific picture of how you think your life or other people's situations should look

You must interpret the pictures you see in your mind's eye

Best psychic sense for creating a believable impression -- *i.e.,* "seeing is believing"

May get confused thinking what you visualize is your imagination rather than guidance from your soul

So focused on appearance you may miss the underlying feelings or emotions

Energy center for receiving clairvoyance:

1. 6th chakra (third eye)

What helps to develop your clairvoyance:

Relax your gaze and use your peripheral vision to look past a person's shoulder

Have a person stand in front of a white wall and notice the transparent colors of their energy field

Go into a dimly lit room with a mirror and look past your own shoulder

Pay attention to pictures or images that flash into your mind

Focus on your third eye when you meditate

Surround yourself with beauty

Always look your best

Let go of judgment so that you allow yourself to observe rather than moralize or even have opinions about what's really happening

Use an eye pillow when you meditate to relax your physical eyes

Ask your angels to help you see more of what is really going on

Integrate the right and left hemispheres of your brain to open your third eye

Affirm: I SEE THE TRUTH IN ALL SITUATIONS

Affirm: I SEE BEYOND THE PICTURE THAT OTHER PEOPLE PROJECT

When I attended Brown University, I majored in art history. One of my professors, Kermit Champa, was chairman of the Art History Department. He was such an amazing teacher I would have majored in tire repairs if that is what he had taught!

It was there at Brown, while studying art through the ages, that I began to uncover the very useful gift of photographic memory. I could talk about a painting and visualize it in my mind's eye in great detail, discussing it as if the thing itself was right there in front of me.

Nowadays as a medical intuitive healer, I use the gift of clairvoyance frequently in my work.

Although my primary psychic gift is claircognizance (the prophetic gift of knowing), I am able to see in a very practical way -- whether it's visualizing clients far away who I am speaking with over the phone, or body organs that speak to me needing attention.

While talking with clients about their past lives, I've seen moving pictures revealing the details of what has happened to them.

I've taken photographs of angels in and around my studio. You can see the photographs on the Pinterest board My Angels.

You can enjoy one of my photographs of an angel in my studio on the cover of my book *What Is Healing? Awaken Your Intuitive Power for Health and Happiness.*

Chapter 8: The Inner Habit of Prayer

"I have told you these things, so that in me you may have peace.

In this world you will have tribulation. But take heart!

I have overcome the world."

John 16:33

To receive the guidance you want and need, you must set your ego mind aside at least momentarily so spiritual inspiration can drop in naturally.

To me, this is like being on the Internet. You get online long enough to receive the information you need. Then you get off the computer and go act on whatever insights you needed and gained. You make the recipe, go to the store to pick up the ingredients or share what you learned with your friends.

You live your life from this informed perspective.

One important way to maintain your inner alignment is to pray constantly throughout the day. Prayer becomes not just a ritual but a practical tool because nothing gets your ego out of the way better than seeking truth from God.

Your ego is the part of your personality that focuses on troubles: your perceived challenges and the tragedy in the world, which, if you study yourself, end up being the same thing. After all, the world you experience is an actual projection of your own inner experience.

When I take the time to listen to myself, I hear myself praying sometimes almost constantly.

My favorite mantra is the Lord's Prayer. I find myself repeating it over and over, usually stumbling over the words until it feels completely true and clear to me on the inside.

It's almost as if I am tuning myself so that I come into energetic alignment with every word, in which case the entire prayer flows easily from my heart and mind.

Here are a few other helpful prayers you can say for guidance. First, from the Episcopal Book of Common Prayer:

"DIRECT US, O LORD, IN ALL OUR DOINGS WITH THY MOST GRACIOUS FAVOR, AND FURTHER US WITH THY CONTINUAL HELP; THAT IN ALL OUR WORKS BEGUN, CONTINUED, AND ENDED IN THEE, WE MAY GLORIFY THY HOLY NAME, AND FINALLY, BY THY MERCY, OBTAIN EVERLASTING LIFE; THROUGH JESUS CHRIST OUR LORD. AMEN."

"O GOD, BY WHOM THE MEEK ARE GUIDED IN JUDGMENT, AND LIGHT RISETH UP IN DARKNESS FOR THE GODLY: GRANT US, IN ALL OUR DOUBTS AND UNCERTAINTIES, THE GRACE TO ASK WHAT THOU WOULD HAVE US TO DO, THAT THE SPIRIT OF WISDOM MAY SAVE US FROM ALL FALSE CHOICES, AND THAT

IN THY LIGHT WE MAY SEE LIGHT, AND IN THY STRAIGHT PATH MAY NOT STUMBLE; THROUGH JESUS CHRIST OUR LORD. AMEN."

Prayer of St. Thomas Aquinas:

"O CREATOR PAST ALL TELLING, YOU HAVE APPOINTED FROM THE TREASURES OF YOUR WISDOM THE HIERARCHIES OF ANGELS, DISPOSING THEM IN WONDROUS ORDER ABOVE THE BRIGHT HEAVENS, AND HAVE SO BEAUTIFULLY SET OUT ALL PARTS OF THE UNIVERSE.

YOU WE CALL THE TRUE FOUNT OF WISDOM AND THE NOBLE ORIGIN OF ALL THINGS.

BE PLEASED TO SHED ON THE DARKNESS OF MIND IN WHICH I WAS BORN, THE TWOFOLD BEAM OF YOUR LIGHT AND WARMTH TO DISPEL MY IGNORANCE AND SIN.

YOU MAKE ELOQUENT THE TONGUES OF CHILDREN.

THEN INSTRUCT MY SPEECH AND TOUCH MY LIPS WITH GRACIOUSNESS.

MAKE ME KEEN TO UNDERSTAND, QUICK TO LEARN, ABLE TO REMEMBER; MAKE ME DELICATE TO INTERPRET AND READY TO SPEAK.

GUIDE MY GOING IN AND GOING FORWARD, LEAD HOME MY GOING FORTH.

YOU ARE TRUE GOD AND TRUE MAN, AND LIVE FOR EVER AND EVER.

AMEN."

Pray before you make any major decision. Perhaps these words won't feel exactly right for you. In that case, look into your heart and express what comes from your own deepest truth.

As you pray, you will feel yourself coming into the vibration of unconditional love and experiencing reverence for all living beings.

Chapter 9: Prayer Is a Two-Way Street

"When you are in the dark, listen, and God

will give you a very precious message."

Oswald Chambers

Many times we are under the impression that prayer is simply an order of words. We can "fancy this up" - praying at a sacred site, putting on our best clothes to do so, setting aside a special time of day or weekly event.

But the truth is that you can pray anytime anywhere, and as you do so, you open up the divine connection wherever you happen to be, Sunday best or not.

As we get into the rhythm and habit of prayer, we begin to shift our own vibration. What you will notice when you pray regularly is that prayer is actually a two-way street.

You speak your words either out loud or silently. Even if you are rushed when you say them, whether you are by yourself or in a group, what you will actually experience is a feeling of being more closely connected to all that is.

As you're saying your prayers, you may even begin to feel the answer, as in, "This isn't going too well, better pray harder." Or you'll know the answer right when you're done, as in, "I need to leave the house immediately."

Even if you've never considered yourself good at praying, start with some carefully worded prayers. Somewhere along the line, you may come up with your own manner of speaking to God and notice that you're beginning to experience a divine connection.

As you make that connection, your intuitive gifts will open more rapidly and you'll discover yourself knowing, hearing, seeing and feeling at greater depths than before.

Chapter 10: Prayer for Strength

"Be a rainbow in someone else's cloud."

Maya Angelou

There are times when life is in fact so challenging that the only way we get through is by developing and maintaining a strong spiritual connection.

As we bond more closely with God, we can become a source of strength not only for ourselves but for everyone around us.

HEAVENLY FATHER,

THANK YOU FOR BLESSING ME WITH THE GIFT OF SENSITIVITY, WITH THE ABILITY TO KNOW, SEE, HEAR AND FEEL BEYOND THE SURFACE OF LIFE.

PLEASE BLESS ME NOW WITH THE STRENGTH TO HANDLE ALL THE INFORMATION THAT COMES TO ME.

PLEASE EXPAND MY PERSONAL CAPACITY TO HANDLE THE INSIGHTS THAT COME SO THAT I MAY CHANNEL THIS INFORMATION FOR THE HIGHEST GOOD.

PLEASE GIVE ME THE INSIGHT TO KNOW WHAT TO SHARE AND WHAT TO KEEP QUIET ABOUT.

PLEASE GUIDE ME TO BE A POWER FOR THE HIGHEST GOOD, TO SERVE THE LIGHT AT ALL TIMES AND IN ALL WAYS.

THANK YOU, GOD, THANK YOU, GOD, THANK YOU, GOD.

AMEN.

Chapter 11: Prayer for Clairaudience

"The first duty of love is to listen."

Paul Tillich

Our ego minds constantly want to share judgments and fears. We can pray to hear the truth that passes all understanding.

HEAVENLY FATHER,

THANK YOU SO MUCH FOR BLESSING ME WITH THE ABILITY TO HEAR BEYOND THE WORDS THAT ARE SPOKEN.

THANK YOU FOR BLESSING ME WITH THE CAPACITY TO HEAR THE VOICES OF ANGELS.

THANK YOU FOR ALLOWING ME TO BE IN TUNE WITH THE HIGHEST VIBRATIONS.

PLEASE HELP ME TO HEAR WHAT YOU WOULD HAVE ME HEAR TODAY.

ALLOW ME TO SPEAK SOFTLY AND KINDLY AND IN SUCH A WAY THAT ALL WHO COME INTO CONTACT WITH ME MAY BENEFIT FROM WHAT I HAVE TO SAY TO THEM.

PLEASE ADJUST MY SPEECH SO THAT I KNOW AND EXPERIENCE HOW TO SPEAK APPROPRIATELY TO EACH PERSON SO THAT THEY MAY HEAR MY WORDS WITH UNCONDITIONAL LOVE.

MAY THE WORDS OF MY MOUTH AND THE INNER VOICE THAT I HEAR BE A BLESSING NOT ONLY TO MYSELF BUT TO ALL OTHERS WHOM I COME INTO CONTACT WITH TODAY.

THANK YOU, GOD, THANK YOU, GOD, THANK YOU, GOD.

AMEN.

Chapter 12: Prayer for Claircognizance

"I always wonder why birds stay in the same place when they can fly anywhere on the earth. Then I ask myself the same question."

Harun Yahya

Often we think we know what's really going on but have a limited viewpoint.

We can pray to go past our accumulated knowledge into the light of true understanding.

HEAVENLY FATHER,

THANK YOU SO MUCH FOR BLESSING ME WITH THE ABILITY TO KNOW WHAT NEEDS TO BE KNOWN IN ANY SITUATION I HAVE TO DEAL WITH TODAY.

PLEASE BLESS ME WITH THE KNOWLEDGE THAT LEADS ME AND ALL OTHERS TO THEIR HIGHEST GOOD.

ALLOW ME TO USE THIS GIFT TO LIFT UP EVERYONE WITH WHOM I COME INTO CONTACT TODAY.

AS THIS INFORMATION COMES TO ME, BLESS ME WITH THE ABILITY TO TRANSLATE THIS TO OTHERS IN SUCH A WAY THAT THEY CAN EASILY COMPREHEND AND PUT IT TO GOOD USE IN THEIR LIVES.

HELP ME TO KNOW WHEN TO SHARE MY INSIGHTS AND ALSO WHEN TO HOLD MY TONGUE AND USE THIS INSIGHT QUIETLY FOR MY OWN BENEFIT WITHOUT DISTURBING THE LIFE EXPERIENCE OF OTHERS.

THANK YOU FOR MAKING ME AN INSTRUMENT OF THY PEACE.

THANK YOU, GOD, THANK YOU, GOD, THANK YOU, GOD.

AMEN.

Chapter 13: Prayer for Clairsentience

"Nothing is so strong as gentleness, nothing so gentle as real strength."

Sitting Bull

Our own emotions can sway our judgment to the point of utter confusion.

We can pray for greater clarity and discernment so that we know what feelings belong to us and what come from others.

HEAVENLY FATHER,

THANK YOU SO MUCH FOR BLESSING ME WITH THIS FINE-TUNED INSTRUMENT WHO IS MY SOUL.

THANK YOU FOR BLESSING ME WITH THE CAPACITY TO FEEL SO DEEPLY.

PLEASE GIVE ME THE STRENGTH TO HANDLE ALL THE ENERGY AND EMOTIONS THAT I FEEL TODAY.

ALLOW ME TO REMAIN DEEPLY AT PEACE AS I SENSE THE ENERGY IN MY OWN BODY AND THE WORLD AROUND ME.

PLEASE GUIDE ME TO KNOW AND EXPERIENCE TRUE PEACE AS I ACCESS THIS INFORMATION.

BLESS ME WITH THE DISCERNMENT TO UNDERSTAND WHAT TO DO WITH THE INFORMATION I RECEIVE, TO KNOW WHAT IS MY OWN ENERGY AND EMOTIONS AND TO LET GO OF ALL THE FEELINGS THAT ARE NOT FOR MY HIGHEST GOOD.

AS I FEEL THE WORLD, MAY THE WORLD BE BLESSED THROUGH ME.

ALLOW ME TO AMPLIFY THE HIGHEST AND BEST SO THAT ALL THOSE WHO COME INTO MY PRESENCE MAY BE LIFTED UP AND FEEL BLESSED ALSO.

THANK YOU, GOD, THANK YOU, GOD, THANK YOU, GOD.

AMEN.

Chapter 14: Prayer for Clairvoyance

"Oh great spirit, let me learn the lessons you have

hidden in every leaf and rock."

Chief Yellow Lark

We can see with our physical eyes a very small part of the universe at any one point in time. But we can pray to open our soul sight.

HEAVENLY FATHER,

THANK YOU FOR BLESSING ME WITH THE ABILITY TO SEE WHAT NEEDS TO BE SEEN.

THANK YOU FOR BLESSING ME WITH THE CAPACITY TO SEE BOTH THE BIG PICTURE AND THE DETAILS AT THE SAME TIME, TO SEE WHAT NEEDS TO BE SEEN EVEN IF IT APPEARS ON THE SURFACE TO BE HIDDEN.

THANK YOU FOR BLESSING ME WITH THE ABILITY TO SEE THE BEST IN OTHERS AND SHOW THEM THEIR OWN TRUE POTENTIAL.

PLEASE GUIDE ME SO THAT I DO NOT GET STUCK IN OTHER PEOPLE'S PROJECTIONS OF WHAT THEY WOULD WANT ME TO SEE.

PLEASE SHOW ME WHAT YOU WOULD LIKE ME TO SEE ABOUT ALL PEOPLE, PLACES, AND SITUATIONS THAT I COME INTO CONTACT WITH TODAY.

THANK YOU FOR MAKING MY INNER VISION SO CLEAR.

SHOW ME YOUR WAY.

THANK YOU, GOD, THANK YOU, GOD, THANK YOU, GOD.

AMEN.

Chapter 15: The Age of Innocence Is Truly Over

"Rather than love, than money, than fame, give me truth."

Henry David Thoreau

In the past, you may have been able to tell yourself:

You didn't know enough.

You weren't good enough.

You lacked the proper tools to move ahead in your life.

Although you may have bought into the idea that you lacked information, that somehow you weren't good enough and didn't have the resources to better your situation, now you know that is not the truth.

Instead of telling yourself that you don't know enough, you can now ask for guidance about what step to take next. Even if you can't see the whole road ahead, you can ask for the one step that will lead you forward.

Instead of telling yourself you aren't good enough, you now know that you are meant to be you in this lifetime, that only you can offer your specific unique vibration and that you don't need to be anybody else or even better than anybody else. All you really have to do is be YOU!

Give yourself permission to let your true soul shine.

Instead of telling yourself that you lack the proper tools to move ahead in your life, you now know that all you really have to do is ask for guidance. Just by asking for your one next step, you can give yourself permission to be divinely led to the people, places and resources that will allow you to move forward.

The age of innocence is truly over because you can step into your power now, using the divine tools of your intuitive gifts.

HEAVENLY FATHER,

THANK YOU FOR BLESSING ME WITH THE KNOWLEDGE OF MY TRUE SOUL GIFTS.

NOW GIVE ME THE COURAGE AND CONFIDENCE TO STEP INTO MY POWER AND TAKE ADVANTAGE OF WHAT MY SOUL KNOWS, WHAT MY SOUL CAN SEE, WHAT MY SOUL FEELS AND WHAT MY SOUL HEARS.

ALLOW ME TO MOVE IN THE DIVINE DIRECTION BY GRACE IN PERFECT TIMING.

THANK YOU, GOD, THANK YOU, GOD, THANK YOU, GOD.

AMEN.

Section Three:

LISTENING WITH LOVE

Chapter 1: Ask Your Ancestors and Never Feel Alone Again

"Walking, I am listening to a deeper way.

Suddenly all my ancestors are behind me. Be still, they
say.

Watch and listen. You are the result of the love of
thousands."

Linda Hogan

Oftentimes we feel overwhelmed with the stress of life and unsure about whom to trust for guidance.

Whether you recognize it or not, you always have a huge reservoir of love, wisdom and support available to you any time of day or night, no phone call required.

You never really have to feel lonely ever again because you can always call on the spirits of your ancestors.

I use this resource myself when I am particularly upset and unable to achieve the clarity of mind necessary to talk to my angels.

What's the difference?

To listen to your angels, you need to be in neutral -- a place in your mind that encompasses total peace without projection or emotions.

Sometimes we feel so disturbed that the truth of the matter is we aren't capable of being neutral right now. We are doing the best we can, but our grief, anger, shock, fear or other emergency emotions have locked us down.

This procedure is similar to a Seven Generation Healing I perform with many clients.

Here's how to call on your ancestors for guidance:

Step One. Clear your energy as much as possible. Even if you are extremely upset, get to the best emotional state you can find. As you know, I like to pass my hands over my head three times while saying, "I clear my energy in the name of God the father, Jesus the son and the Holy Ghost." Sometimes the best you can do is just get 2 percent calmer not all the way, but a bit better.

Step Two. Stand up in the middle of a room where you will be able to walk backward safely without falling over anything. Decide whether you are going back through your mother's or your father's predecessors. Sometimes you need the shrewdness of women. Other times you need the discernment of men. Whether you choose the yin or the yang energy, allow yourself to be drawn to those who can be most helpful at this time.

Step Three. Say a short prayer:

DEAR GOD,

I CALL ON THE SPIRITS OF MY ANCESTORS AT THIS TIME FOR LOVE, SUPPORT AND GUIDANCE.

THANK YOU, GOD, THANK YOU, GOD, THANK YOU, GOD.

AMEN.

Step Four. Ask your question. Make your inquiry as clear and as tightly focused as possible. When emotions entangle our thoughts, being totally sure of what to ask may be a bit difficult. A good way to begin may be:

BELOVED ANCESTORS, I AM SEEKING YOUR GUIDANCE RIGHT NOW ABOUT [THE SUBJECT]. PLEASE HELP ME KNOW, SEE, FEEL, AND HEAR THE RIGHT WAY.

Step Five. Step backward one step. If you have chosen to go back through your mother's lineage, begin with your mother. If you have chosen to go back through your forefathers, begin with your father. Whether your mother or father is still alive doesn't matter because you can always have a soul-to-soul conversation.

DEAR MOTHER/FATHER, PLEASE GUIDE ME AT THIS TIME.

Listen. Be quiet. Allow your soul to receive.

Step Six. When the soul of your mother or father has completed her or his report, take one step back. You will now be with your maternal grandmother or paternal grandfather. Inquire again.

Step Seven. Take another step back to be with your great-grandmother or your great-grandfather. After you have received their insight, keep stepping back one generation at a time until you've gone back through seven generations -- all the way to your great-great-great-great-great-grandmother or your great-great-great-great-great-grandfather.

Step Eight. After you have accepted their advice, step forward one step at a time and express your appreciation to each person. As you express your gratitude, feel their unconditional love embracing you.

Even if you never met your ancestors, you carry their DNA, which means you carry a little bit of each one in every cell of your body.

If you stop for a moment to ponder all they lived through -- war, famine, migration, moving from one continent to the other, raising families, working in all kinds of professions -- you can marvel at the inner strength you carry.

By the time you get to your great-great-great-great-great-grandmother or great-great-great-great-great-grandfather, you are speaking to the source of 3.125 percent of your DNA.

Personally, I often turn to my grandmothers and grandfathers when I feel the most dejected because I know they will find a way to reassure me.

Talk to your ancestors and never feel lonely again.

Chapter 2: Warning: Part of Your Brain Is Not Your Friend

"The best people possess a feeling for beauty, the courage to take risks, the discipline to tell the truth, the capacity for sacrifice. Ironically, their virtues make them vulnerable: they are often wounded, sometimes destroyed."

Ernest Hemingway

Many people mistakenly believe that all their best decisions happen in the brain. That is only partially true.

When you operate out of your frontal lobes, you behave in a socially acceptable manner and access the wisdom you have spent years accumulating.

On the other hand, there is a part of your brain that is NOT your friend and when this part of your grey matter takes over, boy, you are in deep trouble.

What is this dangerous part of your brain?

It's your amygdala, or more specifically your amygdalae because there are two of them.

These are the "fight, flight or freeze" parts of your brain.

All day long I communicate with what I refer to as actual humans -- *i.e.*, not the ones with advanced neuroscience degrees -- so this is how I like to explain your amygdalae to regular folks.

The amygdalae are like an airport control tower, which decides whether you're going to land on Runway A or Runway B. When information comes into the brain, the tiny football-shaped amygdalae send it to either Runway A, your frontal lobes, where you then can think logically, or Runway B, the back of your brain, your reptilian brain, where you simply react based on old subconscious programming.

You fight.

You flee.

Or you freeze.

When I am doing medical intuitive healing, I always check the emotions that are running your issues. When your amygdalae send you to the back of your brain into your reptilian self, the primary emotions are:

- Fear
- Anger
- Shame
- Sadness
- Disgust
- Surprise

To read a chart that I use in my medical intuitive healing to determine the emotions in the amygdalae, you can visit my Pinterest board called Medical Intuitive.

Personally, I like to think of emotions like colors. There are primary colors and all kinds of variations in between.

The point is that when you become fearful, angry, ashamed, sad, disgusted or surprised, your amygdalae hijack your higher self -- the one who wants to be wise, careful, discerning, intuitive and helpful and make good decisions. As a result, you act more or less like an idiot.

You can't be intuitive when you are the subject of an "amygdalae hijacking" because you aren't operating out of your higher self. You are operating out of your cave-person self.

You sometimes can't even remember what the heck you learned on a certain subject. You could have spent years in school and decades practicing your craft, but when you become highly emotional, all that wisdom goes out the window because you can't access it.

We've all had this experience. Sometimes when I become highly stressed, I have to remind myself to breathe -- even though I've taught yoga for 19 years and know full well how to do so.

If you want to be intuitive, you have to begin by operating out of your spiritual self. And that means you want to get a hold of your stress, calm down and not only breathe but make space in your life where you can access your higher guidance.

Give yourself permission to take life a little easier and you'll find yourself making really brilliant decisions.

Surprise! You feel better, mentally and physically, and you can not only think straight but your guidance comes through easily in the space you've created to breathe and feel.

Chapter 3: To Know You Is to Love You

"I listen with love to my inner voice."

Louise Hay

One of the blocks that may keep you from opening up to your soul messages is feeling afraid of what you may hear, see, know or feel. If you feel afraid of your own guidance, that's a sign you don't have a very good connection to who you really are.

You are a beautiful, timeless, strong, eternal, blessed soul. You are loved unconditionally. I know from personal experience that you are guided every step and every minute of every day if you only stop and listen.

You can release your fear of what may come to you intuitively by developing a healthier relationship with yourself.

All the connections you have in your life -- with other people, your life partner, your mother, father, brother, sister, son, daughter, food, money, your boss, your body and even your own soul -- the well-being of each and every one of those liaisons stems directly from the core relationship you have with yourself.

Putting it quite simply, if you don't have a healthy connection to your true self, you may feel afraid of what your intuition could reveal.

If you don't believe that to know you is to love you, you may be keeping other people, your own feelings and even life itself at arm's length. You hide and feel more comfortable with the facade and are much less at ease with looking behind the curtain.

What are the core dramas that keep you from enjoying a healthy relationship with yourself?

Victim. "Poor me" is always talking about being too busy, too tired. You decide you're the victim of circumstances beyond your control. You feel sorry for yourself and therefore think others should, too. You believe you're too weak, too sensitive to experience the truth. There's a limit to what you think you can handle.

Interrogator. Where were you on the night of Friday the 13th? Why doesn't your life look perfect yet? What's wrong with you anyway? You beat up on yourself. Even if you manage to fix one problem, there's always another reason to berate yourself, smart aleck.

Intimidator. You threaten yourself a lot: "Get this done by next week or you're finished!" You are your own worst bully beating up on the part of you that may actually need kindness, compassion or patience. You see the weaker aspects of yourself as needing to be whacked into submission.

Floater. You're aloof. You aren't really home to your body, mind or spirit. You act like you don't really care about yourself. You don't care, so why should anyone else

-- even God or your angels -- give a damn about you, much less guide your every step?

You can begin to get a clue about your own core drama(s) by listening to the way you talk to yourself when nobody else is listening. Another clue may be how you have come to expect other people to treat you.

The truth is that the world we experience is but our inner drama writ large and projected outward into the world.

These four inner dramas -- victim, interrogator, intimidator, and floater -- keep you from clearly hearing your soul's messages because you constantly expect the negative.

How do you go about changing the dramas so you can receive the messages your soul desperately wants to get across to you?

Recognize your default drama. Notice which of the four patterns comes most easily to you. Maybe that's not you all the time anymore. Maybe you've done a lot of deep spiritual work. Maybe your evil twin just shows up every once in a while, but you still want to be able to recognize him or her.

Use the affirmation, "To know me is to love me." Place your hand over your heart and repeat this mantra several times a day until it feels like your truth.

If you hear your inner voice speaking as victim, interrogator, intimidator or floater, you know it's not your soul speaking. Your soul will never speak like a victim, a smart aleck or a bully or as if your soul doesn't care. That would be your ego.

You can have a healthier relationship with yourself when you compassionately recognize that these four ego dramas were just roles you adopted because you simply forgot who you really are.

No matter what you've done in the past, despite all your mistakes, you are still divinely loved and always will be. Step into the truth of this fact now and accept that your soul wants to lead you to greater happiness.

Chapter 4: How to Heal Your Hara Line to Open Your Sixth Sense

"There are only two forces in the world, the sword and the spirit. In the long run the sword will always be conquered by the spirit."

Napoleon Bonaparte

Healing your hara line is one of the most helpful things you can do to access your sixth sense.

What is your hara line? It's a vertical electrical current stretching from above the crown of your head through the center of your body down into the core of the earth.

This electrical current is quite literally your main power line.

Breaks, blowouts or distortions in your hara line trigger many challenges, including:

- Exhaustion
- Inability to discover your true life direction
- Difficulty accessing your inner guidance
- Power loss

Because your **hara** feeds your **chakras**, and your **chakras** feed energy to your **acupuncture meridians**, which in turn feed chi into your **organs** that then feed prana into your **muscles**, you can understand how any disruption in this flow of life force can affect you on multiple levels.

Here is a simple way to understand how your hara line works: Think of a green garden hose!

A garden hose may have kinks that prevent the water from flowing. It may have blowouts leading to water leaks. It may get disconnected at one end or the other, so that even if the long tube is in perfect working order, the water won't disperse to wherever you need it to go.

So it is with your hara. You can have kinks, when it quite literally gets bent out of shape. You can have blowouts, especially at your chakras. You can get disconnected at either your earth connection or your divine connection.

Here is a simple way to heal your hara on a daily basis:

Step One. Go into meditation. Either lie down or sit comfortably. Quiet your mind.

Step Two. Your mind is your most powerful tool. Visualize yourself floating your hara line out of your body directly in front of you and shrinking it. As you visualize this miniaturized version of your hara, imagine that it is between your two hands. Although your hara is usually vertical, for healing purposes you should visualize it lying horizontal.

Step Three. Continue to visualize your hara between your two hands, with your left hand where the crown of your head would be and your right hand where your earth connection would be. Then, take your right hand and gently sweep the length of your hara. Go above. Go below. As you do so, be sensitive to and on the lookout for any distortions in the energy flow.

Step Four. As you gently sweep, set your intention to release, remove or detach any congestion or blocks in your hara line.

Step Five. If you sense any blowouts (think of a nail in a tire), visualize a small patch. Using both hands, visualize yourself patching the hole in your hara line.

Step Six. If you feel or visualize any misalignments in your hara, continue sweeping through. Feel and visualize your prana running smoothly.

Step Seven. Continue sweeping through until your hara feels even, smooth-flowing and healthy. When you feel complete, visualize realigning your hara in your body. See yourself standing or sitting with a strong vertical electrical current. Know that you are connected to the divine and rooted into the earth at the same time.

Practice balancing your hara line daily until your prana feels like it's flowing easily and your intuitive guidance comes naturally to you. At that point, you'll find yourself naturally following your true life direction.

Years ago, I received a healing session to balance my hara line. The energy worker told me, "Watch out. Your entire life is going to change now!"

I have since learned how to heal my own hara. That is why I am sharing these simple directions with you.

Healing your hara line is part of what I do in a typical Reiki energy healing session. Discover how to live in the flow of your true energy and notice how your intuition comes more naturally.

Chapter 5: Walk Up the Ladder to Your Divine Guidance

"This term intuition does not denote something contrary to reason, but something outside the province of reason."

Carl Jung

One of the simplest ways to access your divine guidance is walking up a ladder to your angels.

Here's how you do it:

Step One. Get quiet. Go into a meditative state in a quiet environment.

Step Two. Visualize a ladder above the crown of your head. Imagine that your soul is climbing up the ladder. As you climb the ladder, feel yourself connecting to your angel guides. Feel them welcoming your presence.

Step Three. When you get to the top of the ladder, ask your question. With this technique, you may want to go beyond simple yes-or-no questions. Ask a question from the depths of your soul -- something you have really been wanting to know.

Step Four. Listen. Feel. See. Wait in meditation until you receive your answer. You will intuitively know when you are complete and have the information.

Step Five: After you have received your guidance, visualize yourself walking back down the ladder. Come back into your body. Breathe deeply. Wiggle your toes. Welcome yourself back home to the here and now. You may want to write down whatever guidance you received. Give yourself time to process.

Even if you don't ask a simple yes-or-no question, don't be surprised when the answer is clear and directly on point.

Your angels may say simply, "You are on the right track," or "Be at peace -- all is good."

On the other hand, you may hear information that sounds surprising to you and may not immediately make logical sense. In that case, make note of what you received so that your communications can become clearer over time.

As you walk up the ladder, you are leaving four-dimensional, geometric reality and entering the fifth dimension beyond time and space. Physicists describe the fifth dimension as an extra dimension beyond the three dimensions of space and the one time dimension of relativity.

From a healing perspective, when you enter this fifth dimension, you leave behind the three-dimensional world you project outward from your ego mind.

You also leave behind your concept of time, which seems as if it occurs in a linear fashion, with yesterday gone, today present and tomorrow somewhere lurking ahead in the future.

You leave behind the world you think you know to enter the unity of all existence.

You may experience lightness of being and a quiet inner joy. Even as you are divinely directed, the information you receive will feel calming, safe and loving.

Know that you are constantly surrounded by unconditional love. If this love feels out of touch in any moment, know that all you have to do anytime, anywhere is walk up the ladder toward your angels to experience it.

In this fifth dimension, you are always OK, perpetually deeply loved and constantly divinely directed.

Even experiencing this oneness for a moment can change your entire perspective on what you think is happening in the here and now. From this perspective, you can get a better glimpse of what is really going on.

Chapter 6: A Simple Way to Talk with Your Angels

"Guardian angels guide the steps of idiots."

Nancy Farmer

You can talk with your angels anytime anywhere using this simple communication method:

Step One. First, clear your energy. Rub your hands together to gather energy. Pass your hands over your head three times. As you do this, say silently to yourself:

I CLEAR MY ENERGY IN GOD THE FATHER, JESUS THE SON AND THROUGH THE HOLY GHOST.

I grew up in the Christian tradition. If these words do not feel comfortable for you, call on your Highest Source to remove all negative interference.

Step Two. Calibrate your response. Stand in the middle of a room. Say either silently or aloud:

ANGEL SPIRIT GUIDES, PLEASE SHOW ME A YES.

Notice what happens. You may sway slightly forward or to one side or the other, as in right to left. It doesn't really matter. You calibrate your response so that you get a clear understanding of yes. Then say:

ANGEL SPIRIT GUIDES, PLEASE SHOW ME A NO.

You may sway slightly back or to the other side. If you are unsure of your response, keep clearing your energy until your yes and no are crystal clear to you.

Step Three. Ask permission. Your angels and spiritual guides are here to be your team in this lifetime. Focus your questions on what you are here to do, be or have. With this step, ask permission to begin a dialogue on a certain subject.

ANGEL SPIRIT GUIDES, DO I HAVE PERMISSION AT THIS TIME TO TALK WITH YOU ABOUT [THE SUBJECT]?

If you receive a no, it's not the time, place or subject you need to be focusing on right now.

Step Four. Ask. Once you receive a positive response that your questions are blessed with divine timing, you can begin. Again, this point is like getting on the Internet. You are now online with your angels and spiritual guides. Ask questions for your highest interest and/or the highest good of all. Do not ask, "Can I eat a hot fudge sundae?" That would be an entirely different question than, "Is it in my highest best interests to eat a hot fudge sundae at this time?"

Step Five. Continue asking questions in a yes-or-no manner. This is Angel Communications 101 as you are asking simple yes-and-no questions. One question may lead to another. When you feel complete, ask:

IS THERE ANYTHING ELSE I NEED TO KNOW FROM YOU AT THIS TIME?

If you receive a no, your download is complete. If you receive a yes, then continue asking questions as there is more to be revealed to you.

Your angels and spiritual guides are high-vibration beings who already know your answers. You can trust them to lead you to your highest good.

You are always guided and protected, loved unconditionally and never alone.

I have taught countless clients how to communicate with their angels. Whenever I find someone who is feeling alone, abandoned, neglected or depressed, I like to teach them this simple technique.

Once you talk with your angels, you will never feel truly alone ever again in this lifetime.

Chapter 7: Five Simple Techniques to Muscle Test Yourself

"If you don't listen to that gentle, yet persistent

voice within, you betray yourself."

Tony Sheridan

One of the simplest ways to receive guidance is to muscle test yourself. Here are five simple techniques you can use:

Self-Testing Technique One: Bring your left thumb together with your left pointer finger, making an O shape. Put your right thumb and right pointer finger through the O of your left hand, bringing them together in a second O shape. Say aloud:

SHOW ME A YES.

Now pull on the two connecting O shapes. A YES response should stick together. Now say aloud:

SHOW ME A NO.

Now pull on the two connecting O shapes. With a NO response, the fingers of your right hand should slip through the O on your left hand.

Self-Testing Technique Two: Snap your fingers. Say out loud:

SHOW ME A YES.

With a YES response, the sound of your fingers snapping should   stay the same decibel. Now say aloud:

SHOW ME A NO.

With a NO response, the volume of your fingers snapping should drop a few decibels, becoming quieter.

Self-Testing Technique Three: If you are right-handed, take the thumb and middle finger of your right hand together. If you are left-handed, bring the thumb and middle finger of your left hand together. Now rub the pads of your thumb and middle finger together in a circular fashion. Say aloud:

SHOW ME A YES.

When you receive a YES response, you will notice the pads of your fingers feel slightly sticky and as if they are sticking together. Now say aloud:

SHOW ME A NO.

When you receive a NO response, the pads of your fingers will continue to slip around.

Self-Testing Technique Four. If you are right-handed, put the middle finger of your right hand on top of the pointer finger of your right hand. If you are left-handed, put the middle finger of your left hand on top of the pointer finger of your left hand. Say aloud:

SHOW ME A YES.

Keep your pointer finger straight and push your middle finger down on top of the pointer finger. If you receive a YES response, your pointer finger will remain strong. Now say aloud:

SHOW ME A NO.

If you receive a NO response, your middle finger will slip off your pointer finger, which may bend slightly.

Self-Testing Technique Five. This technique is similar to technique four but slightly different. You are going to use the pointer finger and middle finger of your dominant hand. Cross your middle finger of your dominant hand over your pointer finger, making an X. Say aloud:

SHOW ME A YES.

When you receive a YES response, your X should stick together. Now say aloud:

SHOW ME A NO.

If you receive a NO response, your middle finger will slide off your pointer finger.

Here's the truth: All these techniques may come easily to you, but more than likely one of them will be the easiest. I recommend you find the easiest, most reliable technique for you and then practice it on a regular basis, asking YES and NO questions.

Start with questions of least impact. For example, if you are at the grocery, muscle test yourself about which brand of apples to buy or whether to go to this checkout counter or the next one.

By practicing with questions that you don't really care about, you'll be clearer on your self-testing when it comes to questions you care about very much.

Remember, you must be neutral before you receive any guidance. If you feel FINE -- *i.e.,* frustrated, insecure, neurotic or emotional -- more than likely you will have trouble muscle testing yourself.

Find a way to get to a state of inner calm before you try to muscle test yourself in any manner.

As you ask for guidance throughout the day, you will notice you are easily guided to the people, places and situations for your highest good.

Chapter 8: The Secret to Understanding Your Gut Feelings

"There are instincts which are deeper than reason."

Arthur Conan Doyle

One way we can access our intuition is through our gut feelings. As a medical intuitive healer, I have helped countless clients restore their gastrointestinal system's health. This is usually a two-part process:

Step One. Address the physical issues. These could include parasites, infections, food sensitivities and food allergies, bad bacteria, an imbalance of probiotics, a deficiency of digestive enzymes, impaired detoxification, slowed mobility caused by a serotonin deficiency, and more.

Step Two. Address the emotional issues. Failure to resolve long-term chronic stress usually results in the failure to heal your digestive system, no matter how carefully you eat, how diligently you avoid gluten or known food allergies or how dedicated you are to consuming only organic food.

Your feelings may seem like a major inconvenience at times, especially when it comes to your digestive health. Nevertheless, paying attention to your gut can be an excellent source of psychic information.

Why is this the case? Your gut contains the enteric nervous system, which is sometimes called your "second brain." It contains about 100 million neurons -- more than even your spinal cord or your peripheral nervous system.

Many of us think of our G.I. system as our "stomach," but it actually contains about 29.5 feet of organs stretching from our esophagus to our anus and including the stomach and small and large intestines.

Your G.I. system produces 95 percent of your brain chemical serotonin, a fact that many people are surprised to learn. That is why, if you actually want to be happy, you need to pay attention to what you eat.

And serotonin is just one of about 30 neurotransmitters found in your gut. Other major brain chemicals that affect the way you feel occur here as well, including dopamine and norepinephrine, which give you drive.

Many people are also surprised to learn that your gut produces 400 times more melatonin than your pineal gland. So, if you want to sleep well, it's important to balance your enteric nervous system. Unfortunately, people who take selective serotonin reuptake inhibitor (SSRI) antidepressants often discover these psychiatric drugs produce gastrointestinal side effects that upset the delicate balance.

Because your gut is such a huge repository of brain chemicals, you can learn to tune in to your gut feelings to receive intuitive information.

Learning to use your gut is different from using the brain in your head because you will not access your frontal lobes, where logic occurs. Think of your gut as your primitive brain -- quite literally your gut instincts.

How do you use your gut to tune in to your clairsentience or psychic feelings?

Step One. Shift your awareness to your solar plexus, just under your sternum and between your ribs.

Step Two. Keeping your awareness in that area, think about the person, place or situation for which you are seeking guidance.

Step Three. Now pay close attention. Do you feel a sinking feeling? Does the area feel hollow, cold or trembly? Or do you feel happy, excited or optimistic?

Step Four. Describe the sensations you are feeling in the greatest possible detail. Use words that describe temperature, movement and direction.

Step Five. Interpret the feelings you received. Does the person, place or situation you asked about feel like a good or bad thing?

A key point to understand about psychic feelings is that they don't initially translate into logical information. You must translate them into words and then decide whether to take action on the guidance.

Gut feelings are often the first inkling you receive that something isn't quite right about a particular situation.

By tuning in to your solar plexus, you allow yourself to be guided in the moment by your gift of clairsentience.

Frankly, I believe that many people with chronic G.I. upset have the habit of suppressing or ignoring their gut feelings.

When you take antidepressants, you may be masking or blunting the information your soul is trying very hard to impress into your conscious awareness.

Take the time to feel your gut instincts, interpret them and take action on what you sense.

Chapter 9: How to Stay Out of Other People's Programming

"It's not what you look at that matters, it's what you see."

Henry David Thoreau

One of the most important reasons to ask for guidance at all times and in all places is to stay out of other people's programming.

When you were growing up, especially before the age of five years old, you were easily programmed. You received thoughts and beliefs from:

1. Your mother

2. Your father

3. Your mother's lineage, your maternal grandparents, great- grandparents and beyond

4. Your father's lineage, your paternal grandparents, great-grandparents and beyond.

5. Your culture

6. Mass media

7. Educators, teachers and professors

8. Your priests, rabbis and imams

9. Politicians who make the rules by which your culture operates

When we are little children, our minds take in this information without questioning it. In some circles, this might be called brainwashing, although much of what we are taught indeed serves a useful purpose, *e.g.,* "Look both ways before you cross the street."

Although these well-intentioned beliefs may hold true for many, they may not apply in your specific case, *e.g.,* "Get a college degree, you will get a better job and make more money." (If you don't believe me, just ask college dropout/billionaire Bill Gates.) That is why it's so important to ask for guidance about your own life.

The only way to free yourself from the collective programming we experience as children and that continues every day into adulthood is to ask for guidance about what is right for you. That way, you can begin to break away from what you were taught and find our own true life direction.

HEAVENLY FATHER,

THANK YOU FOR BLESSING ME WITH MY MOTHER, FATHER, GRANDMOTHERS, GRANDFATHERS, TEACHERS, PRIESTS AND ALL RECOGNIZED LEADERS.

PLEASE BLESS ME WITH THE DISCERNMENT TO KNOW WHAT HOLDS TRUE FOR ME AND WHAT DOES NOT APPLY.

GIVE ME THE GRACE TO KNOW AND EXPERIENCE THE DIFFERENCE SO THAT I MAY FOLLOW MY TRUE LIFE DIRECTION.

THANK YOU FOR ALL MY ANCESTORS AND ALL THE COLLECTIVE WISDOM THAT HAS COME BEFORE ME.

NOW GIVE ME THE STRENGTH TO FORGE AHEAD AND FIND MY OWN WAY UNDER YOUR LOVING DIRECTION.

THANK YOU, GOD, THANK YOU, GOD, THANK YOU, GOD.

AMEN.

Chapter 10: Cocoon Yourself to Protect Your Energy

"When you are in contact with your inner silence, you just know what you should do -- you do not have to think about it, and you do not need to compare the pros and cons -- you just know."

Swami Dhyan Giten

If you are a highly sensitive person, you will feel more emotionally balanced if you adopt the daily practice of cocooning yourself.

We exist within one energy (all good and all God), but within this one energy there are a multitude of frequencies.

Those of us who live in urban areas are subjected to a higher degree of negativity and geopathic stress than those who live in rural and more natural settings.

On top of the combined effects of millions of people living together are the individual assaults that many have suffered. If you've experienced post-traumatic stress disorder, you may have actual holes or tears in your energy field that a highly trained healer such as myself can perceive and repair.

Real-life examples from actual clients include a woman who broke her back in a diving accident, a young man who had been raped, another woman who had gone through airport scanners and yet another person who had an unfortunate result from her surgical operation.

You can balance and shield your energy field with this simple technique:

Step One. Sit in a comfortable position. Cocooning is a great way to conclude meditation or a pranayama (breath-controlling) practice. Even if you don't have time to meditate, start your day off right with this centering practice.

Step Two. Bring your hands behind your head, signaling your intention to gather your scattered thoughts. Gather the chi around your head and bring your palms together in prayer position at your heart. Repeat this practice two or three times.

Step Three. Bring your hands behind your lower back, signaling your intention to gather the thoughts and feelings of your lower self. Gather this chi and bring your palms together in prayer position at your heart. Repeat this practice two or three times.

Step Four. Now stretch your arms wide over your head. Visualize the white light of protection. Gather this white light from above your head, fill your energy field and seal the white light below your body so that you visualize yourself in a bubble of white light, knowing and experiencing that you are completely protected.

Step Five. Extend your arms wide over your head again. Visualize the clear blue light of healing. Gather this blue light from above your head, fill your energy field and seal the blue light below your body so that you visualize yourself in a bubble of translucent blue light. Know and experience that you are surrounded by healing energy.

Step Six. Extend your arms wide over your head once again. Visualize the clear golden light of transformation. Gather this golden light from above your head, fill your energy field and seal the golden light below your body so that you visualize yourself in a bubble of gold. Know and experience that you are open to transformation for your highest good.

Step Seven. Know and experience that you are divinely protected, full of healing energy and open to beneficial transformation.

The benefits of cocooning include calmness, decreased anxiety and depression and increased discernment.

You stay in your own energy because you are centered and grounded. From this centered place, you can access your intuition.

Chapter 11: Praying in Groups

"May my soul bloom in love for all existence."

Rudolph Steiner

While you may benefit from asking for guidance every step of every day, you may find an even more powerful experience by praying with a group. Many of us meet regularly at a church, synagogue or mosque for this purpose.

When we pray for guidance in a group, we create a positive force field and align our personal energies toward a single direction. This can be especially healing by raising our personal vibration to match the group's collective consciousness.

Here is a simple prayer we can say when we gather with others:

HEAVENLY FATHER,

THANK YOU FOR BLESSING US WITH THE GIFT OF SPIRITUAL COMMUNITY.

PLEASE EMPOWER US TO SEE THE DIVINE LIGHT IN EACH OTHER.

AS WE GATHER TOGETHER, PLEASE HARMONIZE OUR BODIES, MINDS AND SPIRITS FOR THE HIGHEST GOOD OF ALL.

DIRECT US THIS DAY SO THAT WE MAY KNOW AND DO THY WILL FOR THE HIGHEST GOOD OF ALL.

PLEASE BLESS THIS SPACE WHERE WE MEET.

ALLOW US TO EXPERIENCE YOUR LOVING HANDS IN ALL OUR WORKS. GUIDE US AND PROTECT US NOW AS WE MOVE FORWARD THIS DAY AND ALL THE DAYS OF OUR LIVES.

THANK YOU, GOD, THANK YOU, GOD, THANK YOU, GOD.

AMEN.

Chapter 12: Sometimes Your Answer Is No

"Intuition is a spiritual faculty and does not explain,

but simply points the way."

Florence Scovel Shinn

Like many women, when I was younger, I longed to have a child. The good news about this deep longing was that as I yearned to bring a child into the world, I was working very hard to become a healthier person.

When I prayed to bring a child into the world, the answer I received was silence.

Sometimes we ask for something we feel might bring us the greatest joy, yet the answer we receive isn't what we had hoped.

How do you cope when you pray for guidance and don't hear what you want?

Give thanks for all you receive. If you pray and all you hear is silence or the word "No," recognize that you are still being blessed. Sometimes we can't see the larger picture. Sometimes there is an even better plan.

Know you are divinely taken care of. Even if you don't quite understand just how, know that as you pray constantly for guidance, you will continue to be led to people, places and situations for your highest good.

Ask for your next step. If you've been asking for guidance and the answer you want isn't coming to you, ask what step you can take for your highest good. In my case, I needed to recognize that my life wasn't about being a mother. I now give thanks that I didn't receive what I thought I had wanted. Even though any child of mine would have been deeply loved, my life was destined to take another direction.

Chapter 13: Prayer for Companionship

"It is a risk to love.

What if it doesn't work out? Ah, but what it if does."

Peter McWilliams

Often we long for friends and intimate partners. Use this prayer to ask God to bring these people into your life.

HEAVENLY FATHER,

THANK YOU SO MUCH FOR BLESSING ME WITH MY BODY, FOR MY MIND AND FOR MY SOUL.

AT THIS TIME, PLEASE LEAD ME TO THE FRIENDS, COMPANIONS AND PARTNERS WHO

ARE THE BEST MATCH FOR MY SPECIFIC VIBRATION SO THAT WE BRING OUT THE BEST IN EACH OTHER, EXPRESSING YOUR DIVINE LOVE AT THE HIGHEST LEVELS AND SHARING JOY NOT ONLY WITH EACH OTHER BUT TO BENEFIT ALL OTHERS.

BLESS ME WITH THE KNOWLEDGE AND UNDERSTANDING OF HOW TO BE A GOOD FRIEND AND A LOVING PARTNER.

ALLOW ME TO GIVE AND TO RECEIVE.

BLESS US WITH THE EXPERIENCE OF UNCONDITIONAL LOVE, GREAT FUN, LAUGHTER AND JOY ALL THE WAY TO THE LEVEL OF OUR SOULS.

THANK YOU, GOD, THANK YOU, GOD, THANK YOU, GOD.

AMEN.

Chapter 14: Prayer for My Career

"If you are working on something exciting that you really care about, you don't have to be pushed. The vision pulls you."

Steve Jobs

One of the ways you can be happy in life is to use your talents for the highest good. Use this prayer to attract the right work for you.

HEAVENLY FATHER,

THANK YOU FOR BLESSING ME WITH THE KNOWLEDGE AND EXPERIENCE TO MAKE A

LIVING FOR MYSELF AND FOR MY FAMILY IN WAYS THAT SERVE ME ON ALL LEVELS.

ALLOW ME TO PUT TO GOOD USE THE TALENTS YOU HAVE BLESSED ME WITH.

LEAD ME TO THE KNOWLEDGE, PEOPLE, PLACES AND EXPERIENCES THAT CAN DEEPEN MY KNOWLEDGE SO THAT I CAN SERVE AT THE HIGHEST LEVELS.

THANK YOU FOR ALL THE MONEY THAT COMES FROM SERVING AT THE HIGHEST LEVEL OF WHICH I AM CAPABLE.

THANK YOU FOR THIS JOB, THIS CAREER, THIS OPPORTUNITY, FOR AS LONG AS IT LASTS AND FOR AS LONG AS IT SERVES FOR THE HIGHEST GOOD.

ALLOW ME TO SEE MANY WAYS MY SERVICE BENEFITS NOT ONLY MYSELF AND MY FAMILY BUT ALSO ALL OF MANKIND.

THANK YOU, GOD, THANK YOU, GOD, THANK YOU, GOD.

AMEN.

Chapter 15: Prayer for Peace

"Quiet the mind and the soul will speak."

Ma Jaya Sati Bhagavati

Use this prayer to calm your mind in times of trouble.

HEAVENLY FATHER,

THANK YOU FOR THE BLESSINGS OF MY LIFE.

ALLOW ME NOW TO SET ASIDE ALL INNER TURMOIL, TROUBLESOME THOUGHTS AND UPSET FEELINGS.

GUIDE ME TO THE PATH OF INNER PEACE.

AS I WALK IN PEACE, SHOW ME HOW TO FOLLOW YOUR WILL AT ALL TIMES AND IN ALL PLACES.

AS I FIND THIS INNER TRANQUILITY IN MYSELF, PLEASE ALLOW ME TO CREATE PEACE WHEREVER I GO.

ALLOW OTHERS TO FIND PEACE IN MY PRESENCE, SO THAT TOGETHER WE MAY EXPRESS THE PEACE THAT ONLY COMES WITH TRUE ALIGNMENT WITH YOUR DIVINE PRESENCE.

THANK YOU, GOD, THANK YOU, GOD, THANK YOU, GOD.

AMEN.

Chapter 16: The Intuitive Life and Why I Wouldn't Have It Any Other Way

"Intuition is the foundation of all courage. If you choose to live a courageous life, then follow it."

Ken Foster

Honestly, I feel compassion for people who haven't yet accessed their own intuition.

I watch people struggling along, trying to figure everything out with their minds, worrying, weighing pros and cons, asking a hundred people for 103 different opinions, and I've come to the conclusion that living without intuition is like coasting along without cruise control on your car.

Every little bump in the road becomes a subject to overanalyze when you could simply ask for guidance instead.

Let me share a story with you.

One of my best friends and I have known each other long enough that I guess I've just rubbed off on her.

Recently she took a road trip to Colorado with another friend. They had a blast!

They shared the driving responsibilities. On the way back to Atlanta, however, my friend had planned to take a plane.

The night before she was scheduled to go to the airport in Colorado, she looked in her wallet and discovered that, lo and behold, she had managed to drive for days without having brought along her actual driver's license. Whoops! Obviously, the pair hadn't gotten pulled over by the police so the first half of the trip wasn't any problem.

On the eve of her return trip to Atlanta, my friend didn't have time to ask anyone to ship her driver's license to her, so she asked her angels what to do.

"Not a problem," her angels assured her.

And somehow, it wasn't.

The next morning, my friend took a bus to the airport and managed to talk airline officials into accepting her other forms of identification.

Once she got the go-ahead from her angels, she knew she was going to be OK, and her mind became relaxed.

As you communicate regularly with your own angels, you will come to trust them and develop confidence in the process. Your ability to discern truth from falsehood will sharpen, which saves a tremendous amount of time in every practical life situation you can think of: shopping, hiring people or deciding where to travel, which house to buy, which person to date or whether it's the right time to move ahead or stop and take a break.

Your left brain gradually comes on board and embraces the process because you end up saving so much time and money. Your spiritual tools end up making life all that much more practical and positive.

Section Four:

Cruising Down the Spiritual Highway

Chapter 1: What Does Your Heart Say?

"The heart has its own language. The heart knows a hundred thousand ways to speak."

Jalāl ad-Dīn Muhammad Rūmī

Often we fear that if we listen to our heart, we might lose our head.

Years ago, I went to study in person at the Institute of Heart Math (IHM) in California. IHM is an internationally recognized nonprofit research and education organization dedicated to helping people of all ages reduce stress, self-regulate emotions and build energy and resiliency for healthy, happy lives.

IHM's research shows that the heart's electromagnetic field is 60 times more powerful than your brain's energy field.

"The heart is a sensory organ and acts as a sophisticated information encoding and processing center that enables it to learn, remember, and make independent functional decisions," IHM Director of Research Rollin McCraty reports.

The vagus nerve -- the tenth cranial nerve -- connects your brain, heart and digestive tract. That is partly why when you are emotionally upset, you may experience high blood pressure, increased heart rate and a multitude of gastrointestinal problems.

When you relax, your brain and heart come into entrainment, which means that your brain waves and the electrical rhythm of your heart have come into energetic coherence.

When this happens, you are able to access a high degree of intelligence. IHM reports:

"Heart intelligence is the flow of intuitive awareness, understanding and inner guidance we experience when the mind and emotions are brought into coherent alignment with the heart. It can be activated through self-initiated practice. The more coherent we are and the more we pay attention to this deeper intuitive inner guidance, the greater our ability to access this intelligence more frequently. Heart intelligence underlies cellular organization and guides and evolves organisms toward increased order, awareness and coherence of their bodies' systems."

Given the scientific support for following your heart, you can rest assured that listening to your heart is a smart thing to do.

Here is a simple way to listen to your heart:

Step One. Get comfortable. Either sit or lie down. Make sure you are warm enough. Prop yourself up with pillows so that your physical body can let go completely.

Step Two. Practice breathing exercises for a few minutes until you feel calm. I recommend yoga pranayama exercises for this purpose. You can learn how for free at this link on my website:

Deep breathing is one of the quickest ways to come into entrainment because your breath controls your heart rate.

Step Three. Focus on your heart area. Relax!

Step Four. Imagine placing the person, situation or dilemma you have been seeking guidance about in your heart area.

Step Five. Notice. Notice what you see. Listen to what you hear. Allow yourself to feel the shift in your own energy.

Step Six. When you've finished receiving your guidance, go back to your deep breathing exercises. Wind down by calming your heart as much as possible.

Step Seven. When you are complete, write down your observations. Writing down the guidance from your heart will help you to integrate it because you convert it into language your brain can accept and understand.

From an energetic perspective, your heart may be open or closed. The latter happens when you are punishing yourself for mistakes you feel you've made or protecting yourself from further emotional pain.

If you close your heart down, however, you may be shutting down not only your emotions but your deeper intelligence.

It takes courage to feel.

When I practiced this exercise recently to receive my own guidance, my heart literally shuddered as I grasped the totality of the situation. That is why you should begin and end with pranayama, allowing your breathing to guide your heart back to a peaceful state.

Because your heart is so much more powerful than your brain, you may be surprised to discover the depth and breadth of the information you receive this way.

Open your heart and have the courage to listen to what it has to say!

Chapter 2: Ask to Make It Easy

"There can be as much value in the blink of an eye as in months of rational analysis."

Malcolm Gladwell

As you begin to ask for guidance more often throughout the day, you can make it easier on yourself by praying and asking your spiritual guides to communicate in ways so clear and simple that even you can get what they are talking about.

Say this prayer to make it easier:

HEAVENLY FATHER,

THANK YOU FOR BLESSING ME ALL THE DAYS OF MY LIFE.

THANK YOU FOR BLESSING ME WITH ANGELS TO LIGHT MY STEPS.

PLEASE DIRECT MY ANGELS AND ALL MY SPIRITUAL GUIDES TO COMMUNICATE WITH ME IN WAYS THAT ARE SO SIMPLE AND SO EASY EVEN I CAN UNDERSTAND.

ATTUNE ME TO THE HIGHEST VIBRATION SO THAT I MAY CLEARLY HEAR THEIR LOVING WORDS.

OPEN MY MIND TO KNOW MY TRUE DIRECTION.

ALLOW MY EYES TO BE NATURALLY LED TO SEE WHAT YOU WOULD HAVE ME TO SEE.

ALLOW ME TO FEEL AT PEACE AS I COME TO THIS KNOWLEDGE.

THANK YOU, GOD, THANK YOU, GOD, THANK YOU, GOD.

AMEN.

Chapter 3: Getting to Neutral Is Sexier Than You Think

"In theory, theory and practice are the same. In practice, they are not."

Yogi Berra

One of the major factors that keeps us separate and apart from the stream of divine guidance constantly being showered upon us is -- drumroll, please -- our emotions.

Strong.

Flat.

Jagged.

Our feelings sway us. We project them from inside ourselves out onto the world, often without even recognizing what's happening.

To access your intuition, you must practice getting into neutral.

What is "neutral"? When I first began studying medical intuition, it was explained to me this way: "How many tiles are in the bathroom?" Who cares. Really. You have no dog in the fight. Whatever the answer is, you are OK with it.

"How many bricks did it take to build your house?" Once again, nobody really cares. You are OK no matter what the answer is.

When you get to the point that you're totally OK about whatever information you receive, that is "neutral."

If you are hoping to see something or looking for anything in particular, that's not neutral. If you are frightened of seeing something, that isn't neutral either.

Personally, I like to explain neutral this way: It's like picking up a book and reading the words on the page.

If I am doing a medical intuitive reading, there are all sorts of things that your body may want to tell me, but I have to let the book speak to me. That's neutral.

When we are in an emotional state, our feelings keep us from receiving this direct guidance or taking action on the information we already have.

As humans, we all have emotions -- all kinds of emotions, in fact.

Emotions can shut down any physiological process in the body. They also can charge our energy field so much that we become disconnected from our divine guidance.

How can you get into neutral? Here are a few ways:

- Meditation
- Walking in nature
- Deep breathing exercises or pranayama
- Clearing your energy
- Cocooning yourself
- Not listening to news
- Not listening to other people's opinions

- Setting your intention to connect every aspect of your being to a divine God Source

- If you are upset, calming yourself

- Getting enough rest

- Grounding yourself to the earth

- Praying for insight to penetrate your own resistance

- If you know you are upset and can't calm yourself, waiting to ask for guidance or hiring someone else who can be neutral about the subjects you aren't yet able to focus on objectively

Even though I am highly intuitive and use my gifts in every area of my life, I am also human and capable of getting my panties in a wad just like anybody else.

I recognize when my own emotions get in the way. I know when I can't be neutral. When this happens, I hire a coach to help me sort through and receive the guidance that I need to move forward.

This alone is a special skill -- recognizing what you can and cannot be neutral about.

That is why, when you're starting out practicing your own intuition, it's often easiest to ask for guidance about simple subjects you care little about, such as whether to buy apples or oranges at the grocery, whether to take the city streets or the highway, what color clothes to wear that day and so on.

As you become familiar with the feeling of neutral, you will know when the path to your own intuition is open and when you're blocked.

You will notice that neutral is always accompanied by a deep feeling of inner quietude. This is what is truly meant by the phrase, "Show up and get out of the way."

Your ego gets set aside -- even if only for a few moments -- so that your soul can connect. From this deep well, all knowledge can pour forth.

Chapter 4: Focus, the Essential Skill for Developing Your Intuition

"Intuition is the supra-logic that cuts out all the routine processes of thought and leaps straight from the problem to the answer."

Robert Graves

People sometimes ask me to explain how I do a medical intuitive reading with another person I have never met, seen or put my hands on in another country. Here's the word: focus.

Those of us who grew up back in the day with actual radio sets knew you had to set the dial to listen to the station you preferred. If you moved the dial to 91.1, you would get National Public Radio; 102.3 would bring contemporary rock. Other stations broadcast country, rap, easy listening, classical.

If you didn't stop the dial on the station's exact number, your ears got blasted with static.

The truth is, you always hear what you set your dial to pick up. In modern terms, if I plug www.catherinecarrigan.com into my browser, I'm not going to end up at www.unlimitedenergynow.com, my other website. You can search the Internet, but to end up where you want, you have to be specific.

So it is with intuition.

In spiritual terms, wherever your mind goes, that's where your soul follows. Every moment of every day, your mind chooses whether to focus on the angelic or demonic, on life's blessings or your tragedies, on flashes of insight or reminders of trouble.

It's all available. It's simply a question of where you direct your focus.

As a medical intuitive healer, I specialize in perceiving information about the human body by reading the person's insides (organs, glands, blood, etc.). I scan the body for areas of imbalance that may need alignment or treatment, often connecting the energy back to an emotion or event that's causing the illness.

If I am doing a medical intuitive reading with a person in Germany, my mind guides my soul to that individual. Then, I simply read through the different levels of that person's body -- physical body, energy system, emotions, mind's beliefs and thoughts and finally the eternal soul. In other words, I go into the file and look around. I can telescope in or zoom out to a wide angle.

It's just like looking around a room. If you peek into the refrigerator, you probably won't notice the picture hanging on the wall. If you zero in on the framed photograph, you probably won't observe the dust on the carpet. If you inspect the swath of dust across the floor, you may not spy the leak in the ceiling. And so on.

During a medical intuitive reading, you must direct your attention into each particular area to receive the essential information.

Frankly, I never recognized how much the ability to focus came into play until other people asked me to explain how to do it. At this point, medical intuitive reading has become so "second nature" to me that I have to slow down to explain all the steps.

You may not recognize how your mind shifts from one topic to the next, from one location to the next -- often in rapid succession. One of the best ways to observe what your mind actually does is by the regular practice of meditation. I seldom reflect on how wide-ranging my thoughts have become until I sit down and draw my awareness inward.

The good news is you can learn how to focus your attention, particularly on any subject that ignites your curiosity. The more I care, the more inquisitive I become and the more that gets revealed.

I love taking photographs with my iPhone because the practice of capturing moments of grace connects me deeply with the world around me.

Peering into the flowers in my neighbors' garden, I discover a butterfly. As I witness the butterfly, I admire the patterns of colors across its wingspan, watching its antennae smelling the freshness of the bloom. This exactly matches the focus required for a medical intuitive reading.

Love draws us into the beauty of the world and the wonders of miraculous creation. The more we pay attention and narrow our focus, the more that gets revealed to us, uncovering many delightful surprises in greater and greater depth.

Chapter 5: How to Read the Energy in Your Chakras with a Pendulum

"The person who is in tune with the universe becomes like a radio receiver through which the voice of the universe is transmitted."

Hazrat Inayat Khan

The easiest way to read and measure the quality of energy in your chakras is by using a pendulum.

Chakras are a vital part of your energy system. When energy enters your body, this electrical current first passes through the **bai hui acupuncture point** on the crown of your head and then into your **hara line**, a vertical current that extends upward and downward.

Your **hara line** in turn feeds energy into your **chakras**, which are vortexes of energy corresponding to your endocrine glands.

There are seven major chakras and multiple minor chakra points throughout your energy field. Your **chakras** feed your **acupuncture meridians,** which disperse energy into your **organs.** Last but not least, the organs feed energy into your **muscles.**

If you are experiencing a problem anywhere along this chain, it all goes back to the quality of energy running through your chakras. Keeping your chakras open and balanced is therefore key to your mental, emotional, physical and spiritual health.

Here is how to read the quality of energy in your chakras:

Step One. Hold a pendulum in your dominant hand. Most pendulums have a small ball at the top connected to a chain and a small pointed object at the bottom. You can easily purchase a pendulum on the Internet. Choose an instrument whose energy can be kept clear, *e.g.,* a metal pendulum or one with an amethyst or clear quartz crystal (other crystals tend to store energy). In a pinch, I will take off my necklace and use it.

Step Two. Place the pendulum over the center of a chakra. For this example, let's read the minor chakra in your nondominant hand.

Step Three: On its own, the pendulum will begin a subtle motion. The type of motion you observe will indicate what is happening with that energy vortex.

Here are some interpretations about what you may observe:

Closed: If the pendulum doesn't move, your chakra is closed.

Open: If the pendulum begins to move in a clockwise fashion, your chakra is open.

Counterclockwise: If the pendulum begins to move in a counterclockwise direction, your chakra is open, but the energy in that particular chakra is moving backward.

Over Energy: If the pendulum moves clockwise but extremely rapidly, your chakra is processing too much energy. That isn't good because your system is overworking itself and "over energy" always eventually leads to "under energy."

Under Energy: If the pendulum moves clockwise but weakly, the chakra is open but deficient in life force energy.

Erratic or Uneven Swing: If the pendulum moves but swings in an erratic or uneven fashion, the chakra is open but has an imbalance, congestion or partial blockage.

Your chakras interpenetrate your physical body, energy system, emotional body, ego mind and spiritual self. An imbalance on any layer may affect the quality of energy in your chakras and therefore the quality of every aspect of your well-being.

Putting it very specifically, that means your chakras can be affected by karma or unresolved spiritual issues, your thoughts and beliefs, your emotions, any blockage or congestion in your energy system or physical malfunctions of your body.

If you want to find out more about how to keep your chakras open and healthy, please read my Amazon No. 1 best seller, *What Is Healing? Awaken Your Intuitive Power for Health and Happiness.* It's available at this link:

Here is what you may be experiencing in each chakra:

If your 1st Chakra is Under Energy:

Major illness or injury

Disconnection from the body

Fretful, anxious, can't settle down

Lack of focus, poor discipline

Financial problems

Poor boundaries

Chronic disorganization

If your 1st Chakra is Over Energy:

Hoarding

Overeating

Greed

Fear of change, addiction to security

Rigid boundaries

If the 2nd Chakra is Under Energy:

Rigid physical body and attitudes

Fear of sex

Poor social skills

Denial of pleasure

Excessive boundaries

Lack of desire, passion or excitement

Powerless

If the 2nd Chakra is Over Energy:

Addiction to sex, drugs or alcohol

Mood swings

Excessive sensitivity

Invasion of other people's boundaries

Emotional codependency

Obsessive attachments

If your 3rd Chakra is Under Energy:

Low energy

Weak-willed, easily manipulated

Low self-esteem

Poor digestion

Victim mentality

Poor me

Passive

Unreliable

Easily overwhelmed by others' thoughts and feelings

If your 3rd Chakra is Over Energy:

Dominating, controlling, overly aggressive

Need to be right

Temper tantrums

Stubborn

Type A personality

Arrogant

Hyperactive

If the 4th Chakra is Under Energy:

Withdrawn, cold, antisocial

Judgmental

Intolerant of self or others

Depression

Loneliness

Fear of intimacy

Lack of empathy

Narcissism

If the 4th Chakra is Over Energy:

Codependent

Demanding

Clinging

Jealousy

Overly sacrificing

Giving too much

If the 5th Chakra is Under Energy:

Fear of speaking your mind

Small voice

Tone-deaf

Shy, introverted

Difficulty putting your feelings into words

If the 5th Chakra is Over Energy:

Talk too much

Unable to listen or understand

Gossipy

Dominating voice

You interrupt others

If your 6th Chakra is Under Energy:

Insensitivity

Poor vision

Poor memory

Difficulty seeing the future or alternatives

Lack of imagination

Difficulty visualizing

Can't remember dreams

Denial -- can't see what's really going on

If your 6th Chakra is Over Energy:

Hallucinations

Obsessions

Delusions

Difficulty concentrating

Nightmares

If your 7th Chakra is Under Energy:

Depression

Spiritual cynicism

Learning difficulties

Rigid belief systems

Apathy

If your 7th Chakra is Over Energy:

Overly intellectual

Spiritual addiction

Confusion

Disassociation from the body

I use a pendulum when I practice energy healing or Reiki. I read the energy throughout the chakra system, and that qualitative information gives me a good idea where I need to bring balance throughout your mind body system.

If you have been feeling unwell, a good way to begin to understand why is to read your own chakras. Once you identify where the problem is, the solution will become self-evident.

Chapter 6: How to Read Your Own Body

"In order to heal themselves, people must recognize, first, that they have an inner guidance deep within and, second, that they can trust it."

Shakti Gawain

One of the most useful and important ways to use your psychic gifts is to learn how to read what's happening in your very own body. You can go to the doctor, you can even go to holistic health practitioners, but if you have a better idea what's going on yourself, you may lead them more quickly to ways they can help you.

Here are a few simple ways you can read your body. Start by sitting or lying in a comfortable position. Be sure you have no distractions, and take at least 15 minutes to make a good assessment:

Tune in to your physical body. Even if you have no clue where your major organs are (although most people know where their heart is located), allow your consciousness to roam through your physical self to assess what's going on. Even if you don't know your organs, glands, bones or muscles, you may be able to discern where the discomfort or congestion is located, *e.g.*, on the left or right side or front or back of your body. Pretend for a moment that you have X-ray vision and can take a look. What does it look like in there?

Tune in to your energy body. Your energy body includes your breath, acupuncture system and chakras. Once again, you may not be familiar with your energy anatomy, but trust me, that doesn't matter. Where does the energy feel like it's flowing freely? Are there places where your energy feels stuck? Notice the quality of your breath. How alive do you feel? Observe your personal vitality in this moment.

Listen to your emotional body. With great compassion, notice the emotions that are rising to the surface. You may feel anger running hot, despair weighing you down or lightness and joy providing needed buoyance. As you take stock of your predominant feelings, observe where you tend to be holding them. Are they stuck in a particular area, or do you feel them all over?

Observe the thoughts running through your intellectual body. What's your story? What are the thoughts you continually tell yourself? If you are unsure what's actually going on inside your head, pay attention to the stories you tell yourself about life out there. The "out there" you experience is simply a mirror of the story you tell yourself inside.

Finally, notice your spiritual self. What's going on with you on the soul level? Your spiritual self is the part of you beyond all space and time, the part of you that's eternal and that came into this lifetime for a purpose. Your soul may experience wounds even deeper than your emotional body. Because your soul controls your mind, and your mind controls your emotions, and your emotions control your energy and your energy body controls your physical self, the spiritual level of yourself can bring about the most profound healing.

Chapter 7: How to Read the Body of Another Person

"Art is not what you see but what you make others see."

Edgar Degas

As a medical intuitive healer, I read the bodies of people all over the world. I do not have to see someone or put my hands on you to know what is wrong or what will work to make you better.

Here is a brief summary of what I look for in a medical intuitive reading:

Your overall chi level. In a nutshell, I like to look for a person's overall life energy on a scale of zero, which is completely dead, to 100, which would amount to perfect health and vitality. If you are my client, more than likely you wouldn't actually be dead (at least not yet!) nor on the other hand would you ever have perfect health. People with very high levels of personal energy have generally spent years building their chi. These would include yoga teachers, qi gong and tai chi masters, people into healing with natural foods, regular meditators and others who have developed an all-round healthy approach to their mental and physical well-being. I will chart these people in the high 80s or low 90s. In a medical intuitive healing, I always compare you to a person of the same sex and the same age, with 50 being average life energy for a man or woman of your same age group. When a person is getting ready to check out from this world, the life energy generally drops drastically into the low 20s and teens. Whatever your level of vitality, you can build your life energy by exercising regularly, getting plenty of rest, eating high-vitality foods and learning to take the high road when it comes to interpersonal conflicts and emotional stress. For more about how to build your personal energy, please read my book *Unlimited Energy Now,* which you can find on Amazon at this link.

You can also read more about this subject for free on my website at www.unlimitedenergynow.com.

- **Your most stressed organ.** This is the way I like to explain it: If you take a classroom full of kids, maybe all are behaving themselves except for that one kid over in the corner who acts up and makes everybody else miserable. In the body this would be your most stressed organ. You can create miracle turnarounds with your personal health simply by identifying and healing your most stressed organ. I ordinarily rate its vitality on a scale of zero to 100. Normal average functioning would be between 72 and 85 percent. Overachievers, be aware: If your organ functions at an even higher level, you could be overworking it. For example, if you drink too much alcohol, avoid exercising regularly and constantly express anger, your liver may be overworking. On the other hand, if the rating number falls below 72 percent, your organ may be "under functioning." In this case, I will ask your organ what kind of support it needs to return to perfect health. The solutions could include food healing, natural healing remedies, flower essences, energy exercises or a visit to your medical doctor for further attention.

- As a medical intuitive healer, I find that addressing these two factors -- overall vitality and your most stressed organ -- can lead to massive turnarounds in your personal health.

As you raise your personal chi level, the rising tide of high energy may correct underlying deficiencies.

And as you restore your most stressed organ, it will cease pulling energy from other areas of the body so that all your organ systems can function at a higher level.

To read more about my work as a medical intuitive healer, please refer to my Amazon No. 1 best seller, *What Is Healing? Awaken Your Intuitive Power for Health and Happiness* at this link on Amazon:

Finally, as I read all the organs of the body, I assess at which level your imbalances began. There is a natural flow of energy in the body. I work backward to determine the root cause and address your health issues where they started.

As we first discussed in Section IV, Chapter 5, energy enters the body through your hara line, which is a vertical electrical current running through your body from the center of the earth up to God.

Your hara line feeds energy into your chakras, which are vortexes corresponding to your main endocrine glands.

Your chakras feed your acupuncture meridians, which provide prana to your organs. The latter then supply chi to your muscles.

Because your energy flow may be blocked at any of these places, I take the time to discover where your chi has congested itself or become completely blocked.

Finally, just as you can do when you read your own body, I read:

- Your physical body, including your organs, glands, muscles, bones and organ systems

- Your energy body, including your chakras, acupuncture meridians and breath

- Your emotional body, including your primary emotions

- Your mental body, including your thoughts and beliefs

- Your spiritual body, which entails the part of you beyond all space and time

Having this information can be extremely beneficial because most people wrongly assume that physical problems begin with what they think of as their body.

In fact, your soul controls your mind, your mind controls your emotions, your emotions control your energy and your energy body controls your physical self.

By identifying where problems actually begin, you can clear the issues at their root.

Chapter 8: How Much Life Force Is in Your Food?

"The ability to perceive or think differently is more important than the knowledge gained."

David Bohm

You can tell how much life force is in your food by using a pendulum.

In my work as a medical intuitive healer, I consult with all kinds of people:

- Motivated ones
- Resistant ones
- People who are convinced they know more than I do

- People who want to get better but don't know how
- People who don't care to get better but want to put up a good show
- People who have given up, who have tried so many things that they are totally confused and don't actually believe it's possible for them to heal

When it comes to food, many people have all kinds of issues. One of the quickest ways to resolve the issues with your diet is to get curious.

Is the cuisine you are eating actually going to benefit your health?

Illness is simply slowed-down vibration. Therefore, to heal, you must want to consume high-life-force, vibrant foods.

Maybe you've been telling yourself that you need to eat a certain diet. However, the slop you have convinced yourself is good for you actually isn't.

The first clues that the grub you've been eating isn't actually good for you could be your energy level and the weight on your scale.

Here's how you can tell how much prana is in your food:

Step One. Hold a pendulum over your food. Wait a few seconds.

Step Two. If the food you're planning to eat has a lot of life force -- such as organic, homemade fare full of fresh fruits and vegetables -- your pendulum will begin spinning in a clockwise direction.

Step Three. If the food you've selected has very little to offer, the pendulum will either stand still, move weakly OR spin in a counterclockwise direction. Be aware that any food you put in a microwave -- whether to defrost, heat or reheat -- will subsequently spin in a counterclockwise direction. This is bad. All living cells spin clockwise. When you eat food whose life force is spinning in a counterclockwise direction, toxins are driving deeper into the cells. Frankly, this is the cellular pattern of cancer. Don't go there!

Step Four. Make a decision. Decide right here and now how you really want to feel. When you consume nourishment that is high in chi, your own vitality is going to increase. When you chow down on dead, processed, microwaved, low-vitality leftovers, guess what -- you are probably going to feel rotten! Just how important is it to you to feel good today? Given that it takes four days for food to move through your digestive system (if you're healthy), how you feel over the course of the next four days depends on what you decide to put in your mouth today. So, how important is it for you to feel fabulous over the next four days? I know what my answer would be!

I like to teach people how to use a pendulum with their provisions because then you are totally, 100 percent back in the driver's seat.

Remember, food that is beneficial to you will boost your energy and cause a clockwise spin of the pendulum. Any so-called chow that drains your energy will cause a counterclockwise spin.

That is all you really need to know!

So many people dislike being told what to do by the diet dictocrats -- you know the ones, the people who think they know more than you do about what you should and should not put into your own body.

Sometimes you just *have* to swallow a cookie, or a piece of chocolate, or a piece of pizza, whatever.

Just be an informed consumer!

- Here is a wonderful pendulum experiment you can try in your kitchen:
- If you own a microwave, put fresh water in a cup.
- Check the spin with your pendulum.
- Then microwave the water for 60 seconds.
- Check the spin again.

You may be surprised to discover that even a single minute of microwaving will cause the water to reverse its energy, making it not good for you.

Even if you already have a pretty clear notion about your ideal meal plan, you can use a pendulum to detect if any food has gone bad. I used this approach recently to discover that organic dried blueberries in my pantry had passed the point at which they would have been beneficial.

Maybe you've been telling yourself that the barbecue sauce you grew up grilling with was "oh so healthy." The pendulum can reveal the truth!

Use the pendulum to discover the great benefits or hidden problems behind anything you're thinking about putting in your mouth, and you'll end up feeling better, losing weight naturally and experiencing fewer health challenges.

Chapter 9: How to Tell If Food Is Good for Your Body

"There is more wisdom in your body than in your deepest philosophy."

Frederich Nietzsche

Wouldn't you just love it if there was a simple way to tell whether specific foods are good for your body?

No nutritionist.

No diet dictocrats.

No anoreoxic, orthoexic, so-called food experts brainwashing you about what you should and should not eat.

Many of my clients -- both men and women -- are totally confused about what to eat. The confusion about which diet to follow, which foods to avoid and which ones to give yourself permission to enjoy just adds to the overall negative relationship people have with their body.

They are on a diet, off a diet, going on one so-called cleanse after another and still feeling fat and sluggish.

The truth is you don't have to accept other people's programming when it comes to nutrition.

Gluten-free, organic-only, no-dairy, no-soy, sugar-free, alcohol-free, vegan, kosher, grain-free, low-fat or some other permutation may be what someone else requires to be healthy, but that doesn't mean you have to live that way.

Here's a simple way to take the power back: Just ask your body!

Step One. Stand in the middle of a room.

Step Two. Hold an ingredient next to the thymus gland in the center of your chest.

Step Three. Set your intention. At a deep level, ask to be shown a whole-body response so that you will know whether the victual agrees with you or not.

Step Four. If the chow is actually beneficial, it will strengthen you. Your body will respond by moving forward slightly. Give yourself permission to pause a few moments -- it may be as long as 10 seconds.

Step Five. If the overall effect is neutral, you will remain in the middle. That means the snack doesn't really add value. On the other hand, it probably won't make you sick either.

Step Six. If what you're holding is bad for you, you will find yourself tipping back slightly. It's as if your body wants to move away from the edible item that doesn't agree with you.

Step Seven. You get a whole-body response because your body always knows what is best!

Why is this simple technique so powerful? Because you are biochemically unique.

Recently, I was working with a client who had a brain lesion. For a few months, she and I (and several other alternative holistic professionals) focused our attention on improving her diet. Thankfully, subsequent medical tests showed a significant shrinkage. She was elated!

In case you're wondering how to shrink a brain lesion, part of what I advised her to do was to stop drinking all diet sodas and give up aspartame. In addition, she stopped using the microwave to heat, reheat or cook any food that went into her mouth.

It was hard for her to do. On the other hand, she didn't really want to have brain surgery.

About a month after all the good news, she came back for another healing.

"I feel like I have slipped," she confessed. She still wasn't drinking diet soda and had given up her microwave for good, but she wasn't doing all that great at maintaining high-quality nutrition.

Being a health nut for an indefinite period of time had never been one of her goals in life. Like many other women, my client had issues with food and didn't really want anybody else telling her what to eat.

I taught her the whole-body technique.

She was shocked how quickly her body responded!

I didn't need to lecture her about the dangers of nonorganic food. When we went into my kitchen to practice, her body naturally moved away from any fresh fruits and vegetables that had been raised with pesticides and chemicals.

Even a small container of organic dried blueberries proved to be a no-no (that was my cue it was about five years old and needed to be thrown out).

As a kinesiologist, I've spent years muscle testing food sensitivities, healing people's gastrointestinal tracts and advising them about diet and nutrition.

Another client who has been a medical doctor for more than 30 years admitted to me that laboratory tests for food allergies are notoriously unreliable.

As a medial intuitive, I can read when people need to get this information themselves, as so many people are fed up with being told what to do by so-called experts who often don't have a clue themselves.

Being told what to do dredges up people's issues about authority figures, whether that be mommy, daddy, teachers or other enforcers. Do you struggle to become a goody two-shoes or do you want to rebel, show these people the finger and run in the other direction?

None of this inner turmoil is necessary when you put yourself back in charge of knowing what to eat.

Once you become good at the whole-body technique, you can practice it while sitting at a table.

I teach people to put their hands over their plate and feel how the body responds.

What is healing? Healing happens when we learn how to listen to our body. Your body knows exactly what it needs to be radiantly healthy.

Chapter 10: Your Four Primary Psychic Gifts and Their Chakra Connections

"Love is misunderstood to be an emotion; actually, it is a state of awareness, a way of being in the world, a way of seeing oneself and others."

Dr. David Hawkins

You can open your four primary psychic gifts by balancing their corresponding chakras.

Just as you see with your physical eyes, hear with your physical ears and feel touch with your hands and fingers, your psychic gifts relate to specific energy vortexes.

Clairaudience, or Psychic Hearing, Fifth Chakra. To keep this energy center at your throat balanced:

- Wear blue.

- Listen to music.

- Enjoy silence.

- Write or listen to poetry.

- Channel your thoughts.

- Sing, chant or tone.

- Practice circular breathing and ocean breath.

- Write in a journal.

- Express what you really think.

- Practice speaking from your heart.

- Eat blue fruits and vegetables.

- Write letters you burn and release to the universe.

- Use the G note in sound healing.

- Yoga poses include meditation, shoulderstand, fish, plow, neck stretches, neck rolls, rabbit, knee to ear pose and lion.

Claircognizance, or Prophetic Gift, 11th Chakra. To keep this out-of-body energy center open above the crown of your head:

- Open and balance all your other chakras.

- Set your intention to align your will with God's will.

- Wear hot pink.

- Develop a personal prayer practice.

- Meditate daily.

- Set aside your ego ambitions.

- Cocoon yourself to protect your energy.

- Do breath work such as pranayama.

- Study sacred texts.

- Join a spiritual community.

- Practice unconditional love to all people everywhere, including yourself.

- Refrain from judging people or events.

- Practice compassion.

- See the humor in everything.

- Forgive everyone for everything.

- Practice energy exercise such as yoga, tai chi and qi gong regularly to keep your energy flowing.

- Resolve past traumas with deep emotional and spiritual clearing work.

- Bless all that happens to yourself and others.

- Stay grounded to the earth.

- Engage in a spiritual retreat.

- Enjoy silence.

Clairsentience, or Psychic Feeling, Third Chakra. To keep this energy center at your solar plexus open and balanced:

- Wear yellow.

- Enjoy deep relaxation.

- Practice martial arts.

- Embody and express your personal power.

- Feel the rhythm in music.

- Cocoon yourself to protect your energy.

- Eat yellow fruits and vegetables.

- Develop and maintain good personal boundaries.

- Keep your blood sugar balanced.

- Know the difference between your own emotions vs. other people's feelings.

- Give yourself permission to experience all your feelings rather than suppress them.

- Develop good self-esteem.

- Perform bellows breath and breath of fire.

- Use E note in sound healing.

- Yoga postures include spinal twists, boat pose, bow, wheel, bridge, lying facing boat pose, reverse plank, breath of fire, warrior poses and sun salutes.

Clairvoyance, or Psychic Vision, Sixth Chakra. To keep this energy center at your third eye balanced:

- Integrate the left and right hemispheres of your brain.

- Get enough sleep.

- Wear indigo, a deep blend of blue and purple.

- Surround yourself with beauty.

- Relax your eyes.

- Meditate.

- Visit art galleries.

- Spend time in nature.

- Garden.

- Use full-spectrum light bulbs.

- Create visual art -- paint, sculpt, draw.

- Get enough natural sunlight.

- Purchase a light therapy box if you don't get enough natural sunlight.

- Always look your best.

- Get a makeover.

- Eat indigo-colored fruits and vegetables.

- Perform bumblebee breath.

- Use the A note in sound healing.

- Yoga poses include meditation, lotus, yoga mudra, cow's head, king dancer, plow, shoulderstand, bridge, eagle and headstand.

Many people practice keeping their seven primary chakras open and balanced, but far fewer have heard of the out-of-body chakras.

Experts maintain there may be as many as 26 chakras.

Although you may be able to open and balance your seven major chakras rather easily, your 11th chakra opens as a consequence of deep spiritual growth.

The claircognizance that results from this inner work often has been referred to as a "siddhi" or blessing of supernormal perceptual state.

Chapter 11: Your Four Gifts and the Four Primary Areas of Your Life

"Teach me how to trust my heart, my intuition, my inner knowing, all the senses of my body and the blessings of my spirit. Teach me to trust these things so that I may enter my Sacred Space and love beyond fear, and thus walk in balance with the passing of each glorious sun."

Lakota Prayer

As you open your sixth sense, you may be opening one or all of your four gifts:

- **Your Prophetic Gift, the gift of claircognizance.** This is information in the form of direct knowing, often with no supporting evidence.

- **Your Intuitive Gift, the gift of clairaudience.** This is the reception of sounds, words and vibrations.

- **Your Feeling Gift, the gift of clairsentience.** These are qualitative feelings.

- **Your Vision Gift, the gift of clairvoyance.** These are pictures, symbols and visual direction.

Just as if you are having a conversation with a good friend, you can be plugged in and somehow just know what they are saying beyond the words they speak, hearing their deeper thoughts even if they are not exactly expressing them, feeling the emotions they express and seeing the world from their point of view, and so it is with our experience of our psychic gifts.

It is my belief and experience that you can open all your gifts, but more than likely one or two of these gifts are going to come more easily to you than others.

You may notice:

- You use one gift primarily for receiving information about your family.

- You use another gift for receiving information about your work.

- You use yet another gift most often for receiving information about your body.

- Finally, your soul gift is your primary overriding psychic gift. This is how your soul speaks about important directions in your life.

For example:

- My soul gift is **claircognizance**. This is how I receive important information from my soul. I will just know. This information drops in quickly.

- My body gift is **clairaudience**. I literally hear messages about what is best for my body.

- My family gift is **clairsentience**. I feel close family members' energy and emotions even when they are far away.

- My work gift is **clairvoyance**. I receive symbols and pictures for directions about my work.

Notice how you receive information. In the past, when you've been longing for guidance about your soul direction in life, did you:

- Just know? That would be **claircognizance**, the prophetic gift.

- Hear? That would be **clairaudience**, sometimes also called the intuitive gift.

- Feel? That would be **clairsentience**, the feeling gift.

- See? That would be **clairvoyance**, the visual gift.

When you want information about your body, do you:

- Just know? That would be **claircognizance**, the prophetic gift.

- Hear? That would be **clairaudience**, the intuitive gift.

- Feel? That would be **clairsentience**, the feeling gift.

- See? That would be **clairvoyance**, the visual gift.

When you want guidance about your family, do you:

- Just know? That would be **claircognizance**, the prophetic gift.

- Hear? That would be **clairaudience**, the intuitive gift.

- Feel? That would be **clairsentience**, the feeling gift.

- See? That would be **clairvoyance**, the visual gift.

Finally, in your job or workplace, do you:

- Just know? That would be **claircognizance**, the prophetic gift.

- Hear? That would be **clairaudience**, the intuitive gift.

- Feel? That would be **clairsentience**, the feeling gift.

- See? That would be **clairvoyance**, the visual gift.

Figure out which gift you use most often in each of the four important areas of your life.

The more you understand about how you receive guidance, the less time you'll spend second-guessing yourself and the more confident you can be about the information you receive.

Chapter 12: Show Up and Get Out of Your Own Way

"I am learning to trust the journey even when I don't understand it."

Mila Bron

The only way to get truly great intuitive information is to show up and get out of your own way.

What do I mean by this?

Your ego has this idea that you are a limited, finite human being with access only to information you've acquired the hard way -- by reading, studying, learning, listening to others or practicing what you have been taught in school.

Your ego has this idea that you are an island.

The truth is that, at a soul level, you are an unlimited being with access to all kinds of information. You can know everything you need to know if only you set your ego aside and see, hear, feel and know from the level of your soul.

When I was studying medical intuition, one of my teachers used to say, "Show up and get out of the way."

What did she mean by this?

1. Show up. Be fully present. Be in your body. Pay attention. Open your eyes, listen deeply, feel what's going on. Be in the now.

2. Get out of the way. Set aside what you think you know. Let go of every fact you think you've learned. Accept this truth -- a truth your self-important little ego doesn't want to admit: You don't actually know anything. Be open to what is, to the way things actually are -- not what you project them to be. Stop projecting your prejudices, emotions, fears, insecurities and disabling and limiting beliefs onto yourself, the world and other people. Accept that

nothing is the way your mind perceives it to be. Allow.

Our ego clings to our so-called education: what we learned in school, our academic degrees, the workshops, the books we've read, the seminars we've attended, what the newspapers say, what people report on social media, what our neighbors think, what the polls say, what the scales say, what we think other people think.

Beyond our little minds, however, lies the vastness of our souls.

Your soul is connected to all souls everywhere.

We can pray to access the deep wisdom of our soul. Here is a prayer you can say when you are wanting to get out of your own way:

HEAVENLY FATHER,

THANK YOU FOR GUIDING ME AND BLESSING ME ALL THE DAYS OF MY LIFE.

I AM ASKING YOU TO HELP ME BYPASS MY EGO MIND.

PLEASE SET ASIDE WHAT I THINK I KNOW SO THAT TRUTH CAN BE REVEALED TO ME.

PLEASE OPEN THE EYES OF MY SOUL SO THAT I MAY SEE WHAT MY SOUL PERCEIVES.

PLEASE OPEN THE FEELINGS OF MY SOUL SO THAT I MAY HEAR MORE DEEPLY BEYOND WHAT IS SAID.

PLEASE ALLOW ME TO KNOW WHATEVER IT IS THAT I TRULY NEED TO KNOW IN THIS MOMENT FOR THE BENEFIT OF ALL LIVING BEINGS FOR THE HIGHEST GOOD.

THANK YOU FOR BLESSING ME.

PLEASE LEAD ME TO TRUTH, BEAUTY AND ALL THAT IS GOOD.

THANK YOU, GOD. THANK YOU, GOD. THANK YOU, GOD.

AMEN.

When we show up and get out of the way, we are beyond our fears, beyond our prejudices, beyond our projections, and we can perceive life for the blessed event that it truly is.

Sometimes when we see, hear, feel and know from this perspective, the truth we perceive is actually the opposite of what our ego thinks.

An event that appears to be a great tragedy actually can be a blessing.

A hurt is actually a nudge in another direction.

A wound is actually a place where God rips us open so we can begin to heal at the deepest levels.

Healing happens when we recognize that the world our ego sees is a world of projection. The world our soul perceives is a revelation of great truth, love and beauty.

May we all set aside our ego's fears and insecurities and begin to perceive with our souls.

Chapter 13: Prayer for My Body

"If someone wishes for good health, one must first ask
oneself if he is ready to do away with the

reasons for his illness.

Only then is it possible to help them."

Hippocrates of Kos

You can ask God to bless you with radiant health by saying this prayer.

HEAVENLY FATHER,

THANK YOU SO MUCH FOR BLESSING ME WITH THIS BODY IN THIS LIFETIME.

HELP ME TO BE A GOOD FRIEND TO THIS BODY.

HELP ME TO LISTEN CAREFULLY TO MY BODY AND ALL ITS MESSAGES.

BLESS ME WITH THE KNOWLEDGE OF THE RIGHT FOODS TO EAT, THE BEST MOVEMENT TO EXHILARATE MY BEING AND THE RIGHT PRACTITIONERS WHO CAN BRING ME TRUE HEALING WHEN NECESSARY.

ALLOW ME TO CONNECT TO EVERY CELL WITH LOVE, KNOWING AND EXPERIENCING THE HIGHEST LEVELS OF VITALITY THROUGHOUT MY LIFE SO THAT I MAY SERVE YOU FOR THE HIGHEST GOOD AND EXPERIENCE THE FULL JOY OF LIFE ON EARTH.

THANK YOU, GOD, THANK YOU, GOD, THANK YOU, GOD.

AMEN.

Chapter 14: Prayer for Life Direction

"The door to enlightenment is through the deep

honesty of unknowingness."

Dr. David Hawkins

Often in life we feel unsure what step to take next. Use this prayer to lead you in the divine direction.

HEAVENLY FATHER,

THANK YOU SO MUCH FOR THIS GIFT OF MY PRECIOUS LIFE. I KNOW YOU HAVE A PURPOSE FOR ME THAT YOU AND YOU ALONE HAVE SET ME ON THIS PATH TO FOLLOW.

SHOW ME THE WAY.

PLEASE BLESS ME WITH THE KNOWLEDGE OF WHERE TO GO, THE PEOPLE TO MEET, THE EVENTS AND EXPERIENCES THAT WILL LEAD ME TO MY TRUE PATH SO THAT I MAY SERVE YOU FOR THE HIGHEST GOOD OF ALL.

ALLOW ME TO UNCOVER MY TRUE TALENTS SO THAT I MAY EXPRESS THEM JOYFULLY.

THANK YOU FOR LEADING ME QUICKLY, EASILY, CONFIDENTLY AND IN PERFECT TIMING SO THAT I MAY STEP ONTO THE STRAIGHT PATH TO YOUR DIVINE PURPOSE FOR ME.

THANK YOU, GOD, THANK YOU, GOD, THANK YOU, GOD.

AMEN.

Chapter 15: Admit It, You Don't Actually Know Anything

"Wisdom is knowing I am nothing, love is knowing I am everything, and between the two my life moves."

Nisargadatta Maharaj

One reason why asking for intuitive guidance is so important is that when we are truthful with ourselves, there is a limit to what our ego minds can actually know. For example:

- Scientists don't know the universe's size for certain. They do know it's "flat" -- or infinite -- with only about a 0.4 percent margin of error as of 2013, according to NASA.

- Scientists' best estimate for the universe's age is 13.798 billion years, plus or minus 0.037 (or a few) billion. That means things have been around a lot longer than the mere 6 million years mankind has existed on earth. Homo sapiens, our species, has been around for only about 100,000 years. We simply haven't been here long enough to know everything there is to know.

- The observable universe is the part that modern technology can detect. It's estimated that the diameter of the observable universe is 28 gigaparsecs or 93 billion light years.

- Scientists confirm that 96 percent of the universe is invisible. It's comforting when you can balance your checkbook, measure your weight on a scale, receive your report card from school or college or check out your favorite baseball, basketball or football team's score. But most of life can't be quantified in this way.

- Only four percent of the universe's mass is comprised of the atoms that make up you and me, the stars and planets. The other "missing" 96 percent is made up of stuff that astronomers and physicists can't see or comprehend, including dark energy and dark matter.

- Roughly 68 percent of the universe is dark energy, a theoretical repulsive force that counteracts gravity and causes the universe to expand at an accelerating rate.

- About 27 percent of the universe is dark matter, a nonluminous material that is postulated to exist in space and could take the form of weakly interacting particles or high-energy, randomly moving particles.

The next time friends or colleagues chide you for using your intuition, inform them that you are just checking in with the 96 percent of the universe that can't be measured, quantified or analyzed by any current instrument.

Many people feel afraid of what they don't understand. The truth is that the entire universe remains an enigma even to the most scientifically advanced and inquiring minds.

Give yourself permission to peer into the mystery with your soul rather than your mind.

Section V:

ODE TO JOY

Chapter 1: How to Stay Out of Trouble When It Really Counts

"The power of intuitive understanding will protect you from harm until the end of your days."

Lao-Tzu

As I mentioned in the introduction to this book, in the summer of 2005, I was spending time in a London suburb and was planning to go into the city on a Thursday morning. A colleague had scheduled a day's worth of clients for me to meet for medical intuitive healing.

My friend had put in weeks of work explaining and arranging the sessions. I had never met his clients. Trusting my friend, they had marked out time on their busy schedules so that I could treat them.

As the time approached, however, I had this nagging feeling -- completely unsubstantiated by any outside hard evidence -- that if I went into the city that day, I would have a hard time coming back.

I just knew it.

I had taken the London Underground into the heart of the city on the previous day, a Wednesday. I took the tube to Covent Garden and walked around. No problem.

But the more I thought about it, I just knew that if I went into the center of London on Thursday, I would have a hard time coming back. That was all I knew.

Based on that feeling, I called my friend and canceled all the client sessions he had scheduled for me.

I'm sure I was very unpopular in London for about half a day or so -- until terrorists blew up the subway.

On the morning of Thursday, July 7, 2005, four Islamic terrorists separately detonated three bombs on trains throughout the London Underground and later a fourth bomb on a double-decker bus in Tavistock Square.

There was no way I could have known what a group of terrorists I had never met would have been up to, but I listened to my guidance and stayed away.

Fifty-two civilians were killed and more than 700 others were injured. It was the worst terrorist incident in the United Kingdom since the 1988 Lockerbie bombing as well as the country's first ever suicide-bomb attack.

What is true, however, is that as I had ridden the trains around London in the days leading up to the bombing, I felt what I could only describe as a certain *weirdness.*

On the Monday before the bombing, I was sitting in a train car minding my own business when I felt a huge wave of incoming negativity. I couldn't figure it out. The only thing I could surmise was that perhaps somebody was saying something bad about me or talking trash behind my back, so I drew Reiki healing symbols in the palms of my hands and put my hands up in front of me to try to stop the energy.

But I couldn't.

Even though I didn't yet know what I was picking up, it clearly felt like I wasn't personally capable of stopping the incoming wave of detrimental energy. It was a wave of negativity the likes of which I had never experienced before.

The next day, probably that Tuesday, I was browsing through a crystal shop when I saw two tiny, shiny turquoise-colored pendants.

"I need these," I thought to myself.

Not being exactly sure why I needed the pendants, I found a crystal book and researched the healing properties of aqua aura quartz.

"Excellent protection from psychic attacks," I read.

"Perfect!" I thought. I paid in full and immediately put them on a silver chain around my neck.

Maybe you can tell a similar story about a time when you listened to your soul and stayed away.

I had learned to trust myself four years earlier when I was scheduled to present a two-day seminar in Seattle, Washington. Once again, many people had arranged their schedules to be with me and had put down deposits of their hard-earned money.

That time I had months of inner warning and also plenty of time to argue with myself about what I was receiving.

Even though I wanted to teach the seminar, every time I thought about going to Seattle, I had a bad feeling. So I canceled. Once again, I am sure my name was mud for a while.

This time I canceled with months of notice -- I got that much advance warning from my guidance.

On Feb. 28, 2001, the Nisqually earthquake (also commonly referred to as the "Ash Wednesday Quake") hit the Seattle area. It lasted 45 seconds and caused tremors to be felt as far away as Oregon and British Columbia, Canada. I had dodged another bullet.

Fortunately, you have this inner guidance as well. You, too, have a soul that always knows where you are supposed to be and when it's not in your highest best interests to show up -- even if you are scheduled to be there and other people are counting on you.

How can the rational mind explain such things?

But then again, where would any of us be without our angels?

Chapter 2: Why Stupid Questions Are Bad Idea When Asking for Guidance

"We do not go into ceremony to talk about God.

We go into ceremony to talk with God."

Quanah Parker

As you develop your sixth sense, you may be curious about all kinds of things and want to know the answer to countless questions.

Who is going to win the Super Bowl?

Will the stock market go up or down?

Which politician will win the next election?

Although these and many other conundrums may be a source of endless fascination, they fall under the category of what I would call stupid questions when it comes to tapping into your spiritual guidance.

Here's why these sorts of obsessions fall under the category of dumb inquiries:

1. Your angels form your spiritual team. They help you live your life.   They do not run other people's business and never will. Your angels can give brilliant advice about everything you are here to do, be and have in this lifetime. They can't and probably won't make comments and suggestions or give you directions about anybody   else. So, give it up! Do not try to control the world -- it will only   exhaust you.

2. Work your side of the street. Stick to doing what you are here to do, not what other people are here to accomplish. You can get all the support you need from the spiritual world when you walk in the direction of your own spiritual path. You will get zero

support trying to pursue somebody else's path, so don't even go there.

If you have actual interest in the Super Bowl, stock market or Kentucky Derby, here are some better questions to ask yourself:

- Is it in my highest best interest to attend the next Super Bowl in person? This could be a relevant question. Maybe it's for the highest good that you go there in person -- either to meet someone, experience the excitement or share the joy with a loved one.

- Is it in my highest best interest to buy/sell [name of stock] at this time? You could certainly ask for guidance about what to do with your own money.

- Is it in my highest best interest to get involved in the political campaign of [name of person] at this time? Maybe it is, maybe it isn't. Maybe you have better things to do with your time.

My personal favorite examples of stupid questions include:

- Can I eat a hot fudge sundae? Duh. Yes, you could. But would that be beneficial for any aspects of yourself other than your inner brat?

- Can I lie down in the middle of the road? This is a good example of a totally idiotic question. When you pose "can I" questions, you usually get a "yes" answer. Just because you could lie down in the middle of the road, jump off a bridge, tell your boss where to get off the bus or skip school today doesn't mean it would be beneficial for you or anybody else to do so.

You can learn how to ask your angels really fabulous questions that make a huge difference in your life. Here are a few suggestions to help you ask better questions:

1. Always ask questions for your highest good, such as "Is it in my highest best interests to go to work today?" You are part of the whole. What works for your highest good will eventually bless all others. In addition, you are here to do you, to follow your own path, so asking for your own highest good will steer your life more accurately and successfully in the

direction of divinity.

2.   If you are starting out communicating with your angels, make things easy for yourself by asking yes-or-no questions. "Is it in my highest best interests to sell my house at this time?" Or, "Is it in my highest best interests to hire [name of person]?" Later on you may be able to hear, see, feel or know more qualitative information. In the beginning, though, the simpler you make your questions, the better direction you will receive.

3.   Make your questions as specific as possible and include a time frame. A vague question might be, "Is there somebody out there somewhere in the world who would like to date me?" A better question might be, "Is it in my highest best interests to attend the dance this Friday night?"

You are divinely loved. Your angels guide you every second of every day.

Make friends with your spiritual guides.

I love teaching people how to talk with your angels because then you will never feel lonely ever again!

Chapter 3: Inner Conflict: A Sure Sign You Aren't Listening to Your Intuition

"You are a child of the universe, no less than the trees and the stars; you have a right to be here. And whether or not it is clear to you, no doubt the universe is unfolding as it should."

Max Ehrmann

One thing is for sure: If you don't listen to your inner guidance, you are going to experience an increasing degree of inner conflict. The heat is only going to get turned up on your depression, anxiety, drinking, drugging, overworking and dependence on outside substances to try to keep yourself steady.

Let me tell a story to illustrate my point.

Years ago, I worked with a woman who was suffering from stage IV breast cancer. Personally I wished she had come to me sooner, but she came when she did.

As we worked together, the core issue became evident:

Although she had been married for more than 20 years, she had fallen in love with someone else.

She was married, her liaison was married, and they were in love with each other.

Even though the romance had gone on for several years, neither had the courage to face their true feelings. She even told me, "My mother would rather that I die than get a divorce."

My client was allowing at least one of the 5 Ps -- parents, peers, professors, priests and politicians -- to guide her life rather than listening to her own inner guidance.

And this begs the question: Is it true that parents, peers, professors, priests and politicians would disagree with your path in life, or do you just simply think they would?

I could always tell when my client had been with the man she actually loved because her energy shifted so radically afterward. She was more full of life and happier after she had been with him.

In the end, she died. Her official cause of death was breast cancer, but, in my estimation, I would say it was an unresolved inner conflict.

There are times when your inner promptings push you to go in another direction, often initially scary and outside your comfort zone. If you don't follow your inner wisdom, there is one of only two reasons:

- You refuse to listen.

- You can't follow your guidance because of external control, for example, in the case of extreme dominance by your parents, peers, professors, priests or politicians.

I often feel that people who are drugged up (legally or illegally) should simply take a week off from their medications, sit with themselves, feel their emotions, tune in to their inner guidance and figure out what promptings they have been refusing to hear.

If you've been feeling terribly anxious, angry, depressed or mentally/emotionally unsettled in any way, my recommendation would be to sit with yourself and ask this simple question: "Is there something I am supposed to do that I have been avoiding?"

Maybe you've been sidestepping a huge message that sounds super-intimidating.

Leave your marriage?

Quit your job?

Take up a new course of action even though it sounds totally outrageous at the time?

Your soul is always trying to guide you to your best life direction -- toward your highest good and greatest happiness.

If you don't listen and simply drug yourself, you can feel totally miserable and even make yourself terminally ill.

Why get drugged up, drink, overwork or engage in any other manner of addiction, be it legal or illegal, when you can simply listen?

Even if you don't immediately act on your intuition, just hearing what your soul has to say can clarify things for you.

Your life is still up to you.

Your happiness is 100 percent up to you.

Even if you can't act right now, you can take your soul guidance into account and make a plan to move in that general direction.

You'd be surprised just how much your anxiety and depression will ease up and how much less you need to drug, drink, overwork or otherwise numb yourself if you simply allow that still-quiet voice to drop in and speak.

You don't have to call yourself psychic.

You would probably be amazed to see how much of a connection there is between your ongoing self-numbing process of addiction and your refusal to listen to your soul.

Trust your soul. It alone knows what you are here to do in this lifetime and what will actually make you happy. Have the courage to listen, even if you aren't quite ready to act today.

Chapter 4: What If You Aren't Actually Crazy?

"I thought perhaps she was crazy, but she was only highly intuitive."

Carl Jung

If you have ever suffered the pain of being called "crazy," this chapter is for you.

I like to write about intuition and the way this capacity works because each of us may actually have a very gifted soul. I wouldn't want you to waste years of suffering buying into the idea that something might be actually wrong with you.

I like this song:

"I remember when, I remember, I remember when I lost my mind

There was something so pleasant about that place.

Even your emotions had an echo

In so much space

And when you're out there

Without care,

Yeah, I was out of touch

But it wasn't because I didn't know enough

I just knew too much

Does that make me crazy?"

Gnarls Barkley, "Crazy"

I know all about what it's like to suffer from a label: For years my family of origin thought I was the "crazy" one. Far from freeing me to be who I actually was, this label brought on a massive degree of humiliation and shame.

This supposed craziness eventually led me to accept an official label of "mental illness" and 18 years of prescribed psychiatric medication.

I bought into the idea that something was truly wrong with me. Throughout most of my early life, I honestly feared I might never find another person who would love the real me. This led to deteriorating feelings of hopelessness and many years of desperate depression.

I remember being so stressed and worried about myself that I showed up at my psychiatrist's office one day wearing a cream-colored white skirt, which seemed like a good idea at the time. That was, of course, before I realized other people could see my navy blue polka-dotted underwear through the fabric!

"There," I thought, "I really am crazy!"

Fortunately, I had the good karma eventually to study natural medicine, stop taking the psychiatric drugs (which ended up making me physically sick) and meet people who finally taught me about the way my mind actually works.

Turns out, I am not in fact actually crazy: I have the gift of claircognizance, which is one of the fastest psychic gifts out there.

Carl Jung, a Swiss psychiatrist and psychotherapist who founded analytical psychology, believed there are four primary cognitive functions:

- Thinking

- Feeling

- Sensation

- Intuition

His thinking on this matter became the basis of the Myers-Briggs Indicator, a personality test.

Sometimes I wonder, before I got locked up for 10 days in a mental hospital during my sophomore year at Brown University, if someone had given me the Myers-Briggs test instead of lithium and antidepressants, maybe things could have turned out a little differently.

My favorite professor at the time, Kermit Champa, the head of the art history department at Brown, once told me, "You are the smartest student I have ever had." But when you are thought of as crazy, sometimes that label carries a lot more power than the underlying truth of who you really are.

Years ago I found the Myers-Briggs test on the Internet and took it on a whim. "Congratulations," I remember thinking when I got my results as an INFJ (Introverted iNtuitive Feeling Judging). "Yes, you are psychic."

Not wanting to make a mistake, I repeated the test, only to get the same result. Still intuitive!

The Myers-Briggs test helped me understand why I felt so out of place at times, as less than 1 percent of the population has the INFJ personality type. Jung probably understood this type better than most because he himself was an INFJ.

Even if you aren't an INFJ, keep in mind that half of the types in the Myers-Briggs indicators (ISTJ, ISFJ, INTJ, ISTP, ISFP, INFP and INTP in addition to the INFJs) have intuitive gifts.

Part of the way I like to give back to others is to empower you to understand how your intuitive mind actually works. I explain it this way: "If you own a Ferrari, you better learn how to drive it. Otherwise you can get in trouble in a hurry!"

After reflecting on this subject for many years, I've framed my personal definition of "mental health" to be the capacity to accept reality as it truly is with equanimity.

Discover the truth about your underlying psychic gifts. Stop thinking of yourself as crazy and empower yourself to make a major difference in the lives of others.

As Jung wrote: "Your visions will become clear only when you can look into your own heart. Who looks outside, dreams; who looks inside, awakes."

Chapter 5: Send Only Rainbows

"Can you sense the Creator, world?

Seek him above the starry canopy.

Above the stars He must dwell.

Joy is called the strong motivation

In eternal nature.

Joy, joy moves the wheels

In the universal time machine."

Friedrich Schiller

Many lovers suffer greatly from the pain of being apart, but there is a way to feel comforted from your partner's distant energy. You can maintain your psychic connections over time and space by learning to send rainbows.

But, first, a little explanation about how deeply our energies intertwine with the people we love.

Like you, I have experienced the extreme heartache of missing someone terribly. When I first spent time away from my partner for a significant period of time, I felt slightly adrift and ungrounded, and there was a continuous twinge in my heart. I had trouble eating and wouldn't feel quite myself until I laid eyes on him again.

Once my partner took a trip to Costa Rica for a week. I missed him so terribly I had to remind myself it was time for a meal. "It's 3 o'clock in the afternoon," I would think. "Go down to the kitchen and put some strawberries and cottage cheese in a bowl. Eat something for God's sake!"

Quite frankly there will never be a perfect substitute for being with your loved one, for holding that person in your arms and just simply being in their presence.

But you can practice sending rainbows and activate your psychic gifts so that you maintain your loving connection even across long distances.

When we enjoy an intimate connection with a lover, we form invisible cord connections from our chakras into their chakras.

As a medical intuitive healer, I can read the quality of your relationships by studying the cord connections between you and your loved ones:

- **First Chakra cord connections** show that you consider each other to be family. You are rooted together and draw literal support from each other.

- **Second Chakra cord connections** illustrate the degree of your sexual passion for each other.

- **Third Chakra cord connections** reveal how empathetic you are with your loved ones, how much you care about their true feelings.

- **Fourth Chakra cord connections** from your heart to the other person's heart display how deep is your love.

- **Fifth Chakra cord connections** explain how easily you can communicate.

- **Sixth Chakra cord connections** paint the picture of how much you share each other's vision for your life direction.

- **Seventh Chakra cord connections** represent the depth of your spiritual connection.

The more cord connections you have from each of your chakras to your loved one's energy centers, the deeper and more fulfilling is the quality of your relationship.

If he or she is missing connections at specific chakras, the two of you are having difficulty relating to each other in that area.

Because relationships are dynamic, we can form closer cord connections or disagree with each other and pull away.

By learning to love more unconditionally, we can build stronger cord connections and enjoy an even more fulfilling relationship. The quality of the connections can deepen to the point that we can sense each other's energy even at a great distance.

Here's where rainbows come in:

- **Step One.** Visualize a rainbow from your heart to your loved one's heart.

- **Step Two.** As you send the rainbow, notice the information that comes to you. When you connect heart to heart, you will know, see, feel or hear the other person's heart energy. You will intuitively know how the other person is doing and can be greatly comforted even if you can't physically see, talk or hug.

This exercise works because rainbows contain all the colors of the spectrum. Each color represents a different vibration, as all energy expresses itself through a different frequency.

The fun part of this exercise is, if your loved one is paying attention, he or she may sense your energy as well! This can be especially important if you have to maintain a long-distance relationship.

There is no time.

There is no space.

True love transcends all barriers.

Chapter 6: Amazing Grace

"Trust in the Lord with all your heart and lean not on your own understanding; in all your ways acknowledge Him, and He will make your paths straight."

Proverbs 3:5-6

Even with my own intuition and all the ways I know how to ask for guidance, there are times when I, too, feel bereft, insecure, full of fear and unsure what step to take next.

Maybe you are also feeling stuck -- whether it's about your relationship, your career, your money, your health, your children. You may be facing countless decisions and so many choices your ego mind feels like you've temporarily lost the capacity to reason.

These are the times when I fall to my knees with the greatest humility, saying:

DEAR GOD, PLEASE SHOW ME THE WAY.

It is in moments like this, when life has cracked us all the way open, that guidance can flow in to fill every empty void.

Chapter 7: Prayer for My Reader

"People will do anything, no matter how absurd, in order to avoid facing their own souls. They will practice yoga and all its exercises, observe a strict regimen of diet, learn theosophy by heart, or mechanically repeat mystic texts from the literature of the whole world -- all because they cannot get on with themselves and have not the slightest faith that anything useful could ever come out of their own souls."

Carl Jung

Dear Reader,

Thank you so much for taking your time to go for a ride with me in this book.

I hope you have enjoyed it as much as I have!

I would like to pray with you now on your behalf.

If you like, we can pray together.

HEAVENLY FATHER,

THANK YOU SO MUCH FOR THE SWEET SPIRIT WHO HAS BEEN ABSORBING THE INFORMATION IN THIS BOOK.

I ASK THAT THESE REVELATIONS BE ACCEPTED ALL THE WAY DOWN TO THE CELLULAR LEVEL, BLESSING THIS READER WITH HOPE, HAPPINESS, HEALTH, PROSPERITY, INSIGHT, TRANSFORMATION, MIRACLES AND ALL THE JOY THAT LIFE CAN BRING.

THANK YOU FOR ALLOWING THE DIVINE CONNECTION TO BE MADE SO THAT THIS

DEAR READER KNOWS AND EXPERIENCES WHAT IT MEANS TO LIVE AN INSPIRED LIFE.

THANK YOU, GOD, THANK YOU, GOD, THANK YOU, GOD.

AMEN.

About The Author, Catherine Carrigan

I have the ability to get to the heart of the matter and figure out what will actually work to make you radiantly healthy.

Hi, my name is Catherine Carrigan.

I am a medical intuitive healer.

The average person who comes to see me has seen at least seven other practitioners -- medical doctors, psychologists, psychiatrists, chiropractors, shamans, homeopaths, physiotherapists, nutritionists, herbalists, acupuncturists -- you name it.

I offer a comprehensive system that begins with figuring out what is actually going on with you and then putting together a personalized plan that empowers you to achieve levels of health you may not have even thought possible.

I don't need to see you or put my hands on you to know what is wrong or what will make you better.

I have a passion for healing, and I can teach you how to become healthy using natural methods, including the very best mix of therapeutic exercise, nutrition and energy medicine.

You can connect with me on Facebook at https://www.facebook.com/catherinecarriganauthor

Follow me on Twitter at https://twitter.com/CSCarrigan

Read my blog at www.catherinecarrigan.com

Follow my website at www.unlimitedenergynow.com

Connect with me on LinkedIn at: www.linkedin.com/in/catherinecarrigan/

Keep up with news about my books at: https://www.goodreads.com/author/show/638831.Catherine_Carrigan

Sign up for my newsletter at: http://bit.ly/1C4CFOC

You can read testimonials from my clients here:

http://catherinecarrigan.com/testimonials/

Training in Fitness

- Certified Personal Fitness Trainer: A.C.E. certified in Personal Fitness Training

- Corrective High-Performance Exercise Kinesiologist (C.H.E.K) Practitioner, Level I: C.H.E.K. Institute.

- Certified Group Exercise Instructor: A.C.E. certified in Group Exercise

- A.C.E. Specialty Recognitions: Strength Training and Mind-Body Fitness

- Exercise Coach, C.H.E.K. Institute

- Certified Yoga Teacher: 500-hour Yoga Teacher through Lighten Up Yoga; six 200-hour certifications through Integrative Yoga Therapy, the White Lotus Foundation, and the Atlanta Yoga Fellowship, Lighten Up Yoga and Erich Schiffmann teacher training (twice)

- Practitioner of qi gong, Chinese martial arts

- Certified Older Adult Fitness Trainer through the American Institute of Fitness Educators

Training in Nutrition

- Food Healing Level II Facilitator

- Holistic Lifestyle Coach though the C.H.E.K. Institute, Level 3

- Certified Sports Nutritionist through the American Aerobics Association International/International Sports Medicine Association

- Author, *Healing Depression: A Holistic Guide* (New York: Marlowe and Co., 1999), a book discussing nutrition and lifestyle to heal depression without drugs

- Schwarzbein Practitioner though Dr. Diana Schwarzbein, an expert in balancing hormones naturally

Training in Healing

- Specialized Kinesiology through Sue Maes of London, Ontario, Canada

- Self-Empowerment Technology Practitioner

- Brain Gym, Vision Circles and Brain Organization instructor through the Educational Kinesiology Foundation

- Certified Touch for Health Practitioner

- Thai Yoga Body Therapy

- Flower Essence Practitioner

- Reiki Master, Usui Tradition

- Life Coaching through Sue Maes' Mastering Your Knowledge Mentorship Program and Peak Potentials

- Medical Intuitive Readings and Quantum Healing

Other Training

- Health and fitness columnist

- Playwright of 12 plays, three produced in New York City

- Past spokesperson for the Depression Wellness Network

- Phi Beta Kappa graduate of Brown University

- Former national spokesperson for Johnson & Johnson

- Owner and co-host, Total Fitness Radio Show

- Author of the Amazon No. 1 best seller *What Is Healing? Awaken Your Intuitive Power for Health and Happiness*

- Author of the Amazon No. 1 best seller, *Unlimited Energy Now*

- Author of the Amazon No. 1 best seller, *Banish the Blues Now*

About *What Is Healing? Awaken Your Intuitive Power for Health and Happiness*

In this book, you will:

- Learn how unconditional love can awaken your intuitive gifts.
- Reveal how to open your heart to access your highest intelligence.
- Uncover how to communicate with your angels and spiritual guides.
- Awaken your own psychic abilities.
- Identify the key aspects of a medical intuitive reading.
- Discern how addiction to staying sick can keep you from healing.
- Reveal the blessing behind a mental or physical breakdown.
- Grasp the four key difficulties that lead to health problems.
- Empower your own spiritual growth.

UNLIMITED

ENERGY

NOW

CATHERINE

CARRIGAN

About *Unlimited Energy Now*

Discover the secrets of how you can experience unlimited energy *now:*

• Learn how to operate your body at its very best.

• Master your own energy system.

• Resolve the emotions that drain you.

• Connect to your highest intelligence.

• Inspire yourself to connect more deeply to your infinite, eternal and unwavering support from your soul.

Banish the Blues
NOW

Catherine Carrigan

Banish the Blues NOW addresses:

HEALING DEPRESSION WITHOUT DRUGS using NATURAL HEALING remedies. Did you know that the Centers for Disease Control and Prevention reports that 11 **percent of all Americans over the age of 12 take antidepressants?**

Women are more likely than men to take these drugs at every level of severity of depression.
Non-Hispanic white persons are more likely to take antidepressants than are non-Hispanic black and Mexican-American persons.

Of those **taking antidepressants, 60 percent have taken them for more than 2 years, and 14 percent have taken the drugs for more than 10 years.** About 8 percent of persons aged 12 and over with no current depressive symptoms took antidepressant medication.

Despite the widespread acceptance of natural healing methods, from 1988-1994 through 2005-2008, the rate of antidepressant use in the United States among all ages increased nearly 400 percent.

317

It is my prayer that my new book will be of service in teaching you how to heal depression without drugs, banishing your blues FOR GOOD!

FOREWARD By Abram Hoffer, M.D., Ph.D., FRCP(C) Editor, *The Journal of Orthomolecular Medicine*

Made in the USA
Monee, IL
14 November 2021